OUT FOR A WALK

Anthony "Silverback" Roddy

authorHOUSE·

AuthorHouse™
1663 Liberty Drive
Bloomington, IN 47403
www.authorhouse.com
Phone: 833-262-8899

Published by AuthorHouse 10/30/2020

ISBN: 978-1-7283-6909-9 (sc)
ISBN: 978-1-7283-7039-2 (e)

Library of Congress Control Number: 2020915121

Print information available on the last page.

This book is printed on acid-free paper.

New King James Version (NKJV)
Scripture taken from the New King James Version®. Copyright © 1982 by Thomas Nelson. Used by permission. All rights reserved.

Bryan K. Spurlock - Photography
Desmond A. Roddy - Photography
Shawanna K. Biles - Seamstress for Esmeralda

"Man, it's a great day to be alive"

Walkabout-America...this is a story worth telling. The idea began in Joliet, Illinois 30 miles South of Chicago, in the land of Lincoln. It's a town where Lionel Richie lived part of his life and graduated Joliet East High School. We true Jolietians like to drop Lionel Richie's name for our claim to fame conversations. After my reconstructive knee surgery was when I first contemplated the idea of long distance walking; back in 1995. By the way, the doctor that did the surgery did an excellent job. I incurred the knee injury (torn patellar tendon) during a basketball game in Huntsville, Texas. This injury would play a major role in changing my way of life.

I was at a motivational seminar in Huntsville playing basketball when the injury occurred. I had to leave immediately to have knee surgery. I was on the next flight out just one day after arriving. After the surgery, the doctor told me I would not be able to use my knee in the same way as before, which meant, limited walking and no more basketball. I'm the kind of person who is naturally inclined, to challenge such a grim prognosis. Besides, it's my body, and no one knows it better than me (or so I thought). Although, it was true that the basketball skills were not there anymore (I couldn't cross over or dunk the ball). After eight months of recovery I then returned to my job at the Post Office (PO) as a Letter Carrier. The doctor said my walking should be limited, but it was unlimited from the PO perspective. My knee just hurt. Upon me returning to the PO, they were doing route rebidding, which means workers with more seniority could pick and choose one of the 147 city routes they wanted. My route was one someone wanted; and they took it. It was the only city route in the office with weekends off.

I fell into a deep depression, feeling inadequate as a person, father, and husband. I thought to myself my knee, my route, what next? I didn't desire to use my higher power (God) during that time. I had yet so much to live and learn, and I thank God every day now. I knew I had to switch professions because of my knee, and thinking to myself, the doctor was right. My late great uncle Herbert Mackins came by my house one evening and we tried his remedy of drowning my misfortune and sorrow with some alcohol and smoking. All this did was gave me the crazy confidence to tell him my knee will get better one day and, "I'm going to walk across America."

"Man, it's a great day to be alive"

The alcohol just fertilized the idea and pushed it up for live conversation. After mentioning this idea to my late great uncle he said, "Man! You have lost your Freaking-mind; Black people don't do that kind of stuff." Now the gauntlet was thrown down for me to prove to both him and the doctor that I could do it. It was on (like playing) Donkey Kong. I couldn't wait to prove them wrong. I then found that I needed to develop this form of dormancy and not tell anyone else about this dream. I stayed focused on ways that I would accomplish the fulfillment of my dream. At first I had this erratic thinking, like the wandering flight of a moth, on what to do next. I was all over the place thinking how to execute this. The dream finally materialized after my tour in Iraq and my divorce (2009). This dream would always come up when I would see people walking along the roadside. I would ask myself where would they sleep tonight, what do they do when it rains, how does a person live that way? These questions would soon be boomeranged back to me being the one in question.

"Man, it's a great day to be alive"

My Uncle Herb was only two years older than me, and was like the big brother I never had. With him teaching me how to break the laws and survive in the streets, I was his number one student. With street knowledge and some college it had taken me places a lot of people in this world have never been, and never will go. I thank God for allowing me to be able to experience the ghetto, as well as the educated side of life, and all that is in between. As a teenager, I wanted to step out of the ghetto box and see what the world had to offer, so I joined the military (Army) in 1977 after high school (go Steelman). I was bit by the bug (the curiosity bug), to want more out of life. I found that those old fashioned clichés of prejudice, like don't trust the blue eyed white man, or they won't let you do certain things, was very foreign to me. I was a rookie very ignorant about life and its struggles as a Black man back in the nineteen seventies. I approached life back then like a bubbling puppy struggling to put one foot in front of the other and tumbling onto its face. I was just learning the balance of life. Those were some great learning curves back then; nevertheless, during my adventures with life's journey in those days, they were excellent. I can relate wholeheartedly with the very true notion that the journey is the most exciting part of life.

Langston Hughes once said; *"Hold fast to dreams for if dreams die, life is like a broken-winged bird that cannot fly."*

"Man, it's a great day to be alive"

I often think of that old Tootsie Pop TV commercial with the little boy that goes around asking this turtle, "How many licks does it take to get to the center of a Tootsie Pop?" The turtle then replies, "I don't know, I never made it without biting, you should ask Mr. Owl."

The little boy finds Mr. Owl and asks him. Mr. Owl swoops up The Tootsie Pop as he says, "let's see." Mr. Owl rips off the wrapper, sticks Tootsie Pop in his mouth and starts licking it as he counts. "One, two, three" CRUNCH! It was all over ladies and gentlemen he couldn't get passed three licks. I can recall the joy I had with that candy getting to the soft center. I mention this because; walking from point A to Z and getting all that good stuff in-between has given me that same joy. The people that I told I would walk across America would be like the little boy asking how many licks does it take to get to the center, and I would be like the owl. Taking the wrapper off and saying "let's see how many." Sitting in a stranger's kitchen and eating fried grits somewhere in Missouri, or drinking goat's milk in Depauw, Indiana, gave me joy knowing I may not ever experience this again in my lifetime. These things are priceless. I can remember asking myself, "how many miles does it take to walk through the center of the United States?" Walking at 3mph, you have a lot of time to think, and some of the thoughts are of life events that you will never forget. Thank you, Nestles, like this commercial memory; the commercial would come on and spell these letters out loud;

"N-E-S- T- L- E-S, Nestles makes the very best!" I know you Baby Boomer's remember that commercial jingle.

"Man, it's a great day to be alive"

Every person that has taken the plunge, by walking across the United States has made some type of slash with the, "WHY?" Dr. John Francis, during the civil rights struggles, would be called a planet walker after 22 years of walking. Dr. Francis not only walked but, during my high school years he walked and chose a vow-of silence, not speaking for the first 17 years during his walk with his banjo. This man had conviction with action, or action with conviction. Whichever it was, I knew I had to be a part of doing something like that.

"The essence of America - that which really unites us - is not ethnicity, or nationality or religion - it is an idea - and what an idea it is: That you can come from humble circumstances and do great things." Condoleezza Rice

"Man, it's a great day to be alive"

Francis quoted a man speaking on the radio after two oil tankers collided in San Francisco Bay (1971) spilling 800,000 gallon of oil;

"And if you don't like the news go out and make some news of your own." That moment resonated within the soul of Dr. Francis to do something positive. He took a stand not to use oil or fuel that harms our environment during those 17 years. This was his "why" (helping other people). While I was listening to his epic journey it ignited my idea even more to go *out for a walk.*

Dr. Francis was the first Black American to walk from coast to coast. It intrigued me so much, and on top of that, he became the first person to walk in total solitude for 17 years during his walk around the planet. This really sparked my level of curiosity, reading and listening-to a man with the same skin color as my own. I felt like this little kid looking up to a role model and wanting to be just like him. For the first time in my life it seemed like I was in total control. I felt very strong (mentally and physically) about what I wanted to do and did not have to answer to anyone but myself. After listing to Dr. Francis on a technology, entertainment, design talk (TED talk), I told myself that I was going to join that elite group of people. I imagined this association (people who walk across America) being like Senators or the House of Representatives, NBA champions, or a group of astronauts flying into space. Not many people do this but it is something that many people respect. I saw myself over and over again in my imagination walking and then telling my story on a TED talk like Dr. Francis one day. Well, I did the walk, now I have to speak on TED talk.

"The power of Imagination makes us infinite." John Muir

"Man, it's a great day to be alive"

After more research about the first Black American to walk coast to coast, I was curious to find out who was the second Black American to complete this journey. It could be me (saying this to myself with so much enthusiasm) who could carry the torch. The first Black American to walk on any epic journey across America was Mr. Willie T. Clay, in (The Big Walk), in 1960. Mr. Clay walked from Cincinnati, Ohio to San Diego, California when I was only a year old. Mr. Clay walked to bring awareness to the economic issues that plagued the Black communities during the civil rights movement. That was his WHY. He met up with me in Los Angeles, California in December 2015 after my Walkabout-America. This blew my mind, because he was hell-bent on interviewing me. I kept telling him, he was one of the motivating factors for me walking. Mr. Clay told me that I rekindled old flames about his journey and that I walked further than he did. Dr. Francis (another motivating factor) walked from the West Coast to the East Coast starting in 1971. I would be the second Black American to complete a cross-country journey, this time from the East Coast to the West Coast. Yes! I'm in that elite group with one of my foremost accomplishments.

I would often think, as I walked, how I would rank with the men of color who had blazed the trail for me. This is what I came up with; Mr. Clay was like the granddaddy with "The Big Walk" (in 1960) across America. Dr. Francis was like that great uncle with his walk across America/Planet walker (1971). Then there's me, bringing up the rear, as this tinkering wide-eyed curious grandson/nephew with my Walkabout-America (2015). One, two, three, man this is a great podium to stand on and be recognized with these extraordinary human beings.

I would be remiss if I didn't mention another motivating factor that caused me to take the pledge. Her name is Cheryl Strayed. I read her book, "Wild: From Lost to Found on the Pacific Crest Trail," and I thought it was amazing. It was very inspiring and down to earth. I thought if this lady could walk over a thousand miles and lose six toe-nails in the process, I know I can do this. You wouldn't believe how much it inspired me.

I'm living my dream. I have never felt like this in all my life. The biggest lesson I have learned was I didn't learn to love myself while growing up. Right up to the time of my marriage, and throughout my marriage. Growing up, I sometimes felt forsaken. I used to beat myself up a lot, I would always put myself last and try to please others. Once I learned how to revert from being a people pleaser, to an Anthony pleaser, a whole other world opened up. It was a feeling that I could never be more alive than I am right now, right where I stand. So I'm going to live it, because it's my time to shine.

"And if you don't like the news, go out and make some news of your own." Dr. John Francis

"Man, it's a great day to be alive"

I think that we are all placed on this earth to be who we are and to realize and know that we are very, very powerful. We are all amazing, impressive, beautiful beings. I am much brawnier than I ever thought I was. I finally found a purpose for who I am and what I'm supposed to do to make me happy. The only purpose I have on this planet is to be myself, because that's all I can be, one day at a time. The 12-step serenity prayer goes like this;

"God grant me the serenity to accept the things I cannot change, the courage to change the things I can, and the wisdom to know the difference."

That passage served me well during my journey across this vast country. I had to accept the fact that some people looked down on me as a vagabond derelict when I walked. The things I could change, I did, by granting wishes to deserving families. Last but not least, I would like to thank God for giving me the wisdom to *"Know when to hold 'em, Know when to fold 'em, Know when to walk away, and Know when to run"* (Kenny Rogers), and to know the difference. I have learned in my lifetime how people live in all 50 states as I traveled through them, alone, and to countries outside the States like Germany, Italy, UK, France, Switzerland, Spain, Panama, Mexico, Austria, Japan, Korea, Iceland, Kuwait, and Iraq. I say this because I have an impressive resume when it comes to learning the diversity of people.

Yes, I'm tooting my own horn. I have communicated with so many different nationalities over the years. All this leads to the Walkabout-America.

I think that without having the experience of communicating and getting my point across with diverse people it would have not been as successful as it was. You know with every planned idea, you MUST have a plan to execute that mastermind idea. My execution plan was to retire from my job, do research on distance walking, set goals, build a carrier chart for transporting my goods while trekking across America, build up my upper body, and walk. This plan went on for four to five years until completed. With the building of the chart, I knew I had to come up with an idea to safely carry all my equipment for the Walkabout-America. During my research I found Phil Cihiwsky from Colorado who walked across America at age 59 and he had a modified three-wheeler. From that I decided to use my granddaughter's three-wheeler stroller.

"Setting goals is the first step in turning the invisible into the visible."
Tony Robbins

"Man, it's a great day to be alive"

Mr. Lawrence Medina, my best friend, was the gracious donor of the three-wheeler stroller. After the first twenty miles pushing that stroller, I named her Esmeralda. I thought of Tom Hanks in the movie *Castaway* when he talked to (Wilson) his soccer ball. I also thought of my late Uncle Herb who had a lady friend in the 1970's named Esmeralda who liked both of us. I thought it would be fitting to name my cart after one of my late Uncle Herb's ladies. Proving to him that doing the Walkabout America with Esmeralda was possible.

Bo Jackson once said, *"Set your goals high, and don't stop till you get there."* This quote was very instrumental for me during the push up my first summit in Pennsylvania. How could a person set a goal of such magnitude and it not be a high goal. With my high goal being set, I needed to decide on a purpose for doing such a historical walk. The purpose could not have come from a better place than church. The church that I had been attending in Albuquerque, New Mexico, throughout the years, called Legacy Church, had always been a giving source to many organizations. One particular day during service, the church was having a recognition day for the funds raised for the Make-A-Wish Foundation. The Albuquerque chapter President was accepting a donation from the church and a small girl, around 11 years old, spoke on stage about how Make-A-Wish helped her and her family during some pretty hard times. I was profoundly moved in a way that all I could think about was that, "I'm going to raise money for the Make-A-Wish foundation." I feel that children are our future, whether we help them or not. I like to go with the universal law and do the right thing. Our children are individuals, and each one of them is unique. What affects them most is our attitudes and the loving, kind disposition we choose to display when around them and with others. I think we need to hold on to the attitudes that say, "Yes to life and the world," and you would be amazed at the changes you will see. Children will make you laugh. Take life in a light-hearted way, laugh a lot, be responsible, be orderly, be disciplined, laugh, laugh, and laugh some more. Remember, being too serious is a disease of the ego. The EGO is no more than edging God out. I feel that I was too serious and didn't laugh enough with my children growing up. I had a huge ego. That was not a good thing for a young family. I learned this (not to be so serious) in my later years in life. I have come out of that stagnation, and out of the hatred of blaming everybody else. I have come out of frustration with myself. My sons and I have a great relationship as individual adults. The clarity that I found through my higher power (God) has kept these following words warmly percolating in most of my conversation with others, "Love God, Love People," and children of course are people too.

"Man, it's a great day to be alive"

After retiring, I realized this coast to coast endeavor needed to be financed in order for me to make it a successful journey. So, I went out and got a part-time job to save up a few thousand dollars for the repairing of (Wilbur) my 1994 Mazda B4000 truck and equipment for the walk. I also got out of character and grew this big white/grey beard which was going to be my trade-mark. The guys I worked with at the part time job would call me Silverback, which I used during my journey. That job I had was very humbling. It taught me to have patience. The adults I worked with had special needs. They taught me a lot.

I can remember one particular night in 2014 as though it was yesterday, sitting on my patio drinking some wine looking up at the stars. I would ask myself over and over again, "What state am I going to be in next year this time (2015)? Will the weather be nice or will it be nasty? Will the people treat me different because I'm a Black man walking through those little Andy Griffith Mayberry towns? Would they ignore me and pass me off as a homeless derelict wanting something, or would nothing happen, but a kind nod of the head and respect as a person, and with that we all keep moving. The nod of the head happened to me more times than not. Then I would try my hardest to imagine what states would look like that I would walk through. The part-time job lasted for about six months and I then had enough money to start my endeavor.

I watched the Walkabout America to-do list (hanging on the refrigerator) dwindle, and it was time to go to Kentucky for a ride to Maine. Wilbur was running strong and smooth, from an overhaul, like it just got a shot of adrenaline. At last, the day had finally come. I went into the last day of preparation with an over-kill on making sure I would not forget anything.

I knew I wouldn't be back to this exact spot for about a year minimum. It was a different feeling for sure. Everything fashioned around a human being like me setting goals. We reach our goals; all we have to do is set them. At this point in my life I have reached goals that I have set out to do (have a good starting point). We humans have never set a goal that we have not reached. I set a goal while training one day which was to walk 14 hours with a backpack. Walking with a backpack, and all of the essentials I needed for the walk, turned out to be too much of a daunting task.

"The only real purpose of a goal is to inspire you to fall more deeply in love with life." Michael Neill

"Man, it's a great day to be alive"

It was then when I decided I don't want to put anything on my back, only a camel-back, occasionally, for a sip of water. Come to find out, this decision was a good one, I couldn't sleep that night, anticipating my road trip to Symsonia, Kentucky. I got up around 2:20 a.m. and packed what remaining items I could squeeze into my truck, Wilbur. My youngest son (Wynton) got up and helped me, and to said goodbye. He placed an infantry rifle license plate on the front of my truck for me that morning before leaving. I really appreciated that kind gesture from him, I had tried to put the plate on earlier, but the holes didn't line up. He got out his grinder and 1,2,3, it was done. The holes lined up, the truck looked great, and that small act of kindness made me proud that he was my son. It really helped de-stress me at the time. I knew that I wouldn't be seeing him for a while, and knew I would miss him dearly, right along with other relatives and friends. The infantry license plate was something I had purchased the weekend before from an outdoors flea market by the fairgrounds off of Rt. 66 in Albuquerque. The Army Infantry plate was a representation of power and strength that I successfully completed infantry training while in the Army. The plate also takes me back to my son installing it for me that morning.

In my mind, I was thinking I couldn't fail this journey with what I have learned in this life. Whether it be education, street smarts, military, government job, owning a home, raising a family, or traveling. All these things contributed to my successful, historical Walkabout-America. Then he gave me a gift I thought at the time was strange, but was very helpful throughout my journey. It was a gift of about 15 or so used lighters all bundled up with some electrical tape around them. He said, "Here, Dad, you might need these." Man, I got choked up and thanked him and gave him a hug. It was a sad, bitter sweet feeling which is hard to describe, and will never be duplicated again in our lifetime. I knew this was it. Be a man of your word because my sons were watching me, I thought I had to "Man Up" as Barncy Fife would say on the Andy Griffith show. After hugging Wynton, my oldest son Desmond, and his girlfriend Kim (the mother of my granddaughters Aalyiaa and Hazele) and then lightly kissing my two sleeping granddaughters on the forehead, I took off for Symsonia, Kentucky. There was no turning back. No more working with the clients of Adelante (my part-time job) where I got the name "Silverback". No more Hospice De la Luz, where I would miss my 96 year old girlfriend Bella, and no more training for the walk. This Superbowl of events had now come. I had really enjoyed and learned so much from the people of those two organizations and will miss them dearly. They were the springboard of patience for me, which I used each day on my 244 days historical trek.

"If you run you stand a chance of losing, but if you don't run you've already lost." Barack Obama

"Man, it's a great day to be alive"

The time had finally arrived. It was Tuesday, February 24th, 2015, and with a temperature of about 35 degrees with wind speeds out of the NW at 9 mph. Around 3:30 a.m., I decided to pull away from Albuquerque. I couldn't help but think, "my life is about to change." I kept saying to myself, "this is really happening," "this is really happening," "this is really happening!" I called my sister Shawanna and told her I was on my way to Kentucky. She and I would text one another the whole way to help keep me awake. Paducah/Symsonia is an 18 hour drive along I-40.

I had all my affairs finally in order, and I felt a freedom come over me thinking about that. I say that because, I knew I wouldn't be bombarded with the daily responsibly of figuring out, and or paying bills. This is something that I am going to relish for the rest of this entire year. I think you live longer if you don't have to think about those things like paying bills and the stress of (say) a $35,000 medical bill that you get in the mail. Don't get me wrong, I'm not naive to the point where I don't think we will get any more bills for the rest of our lives, because we will. I'm simply stating that holding a handful of letters from the letter carrier and reading them is not conducive to my good health or freedom. This newfound freedom made me think of getting deployed to Iraq. While away traveling the world as a solider, you don't have the normal bombardment that the civilians have each day (like getting mail or paying bills). So this whole Walkabout-America has given me the courage to stand tall and be counted. While I ventured across this wonderful land of America my two sons, Kim Thompson (my granddaughter's mom) Aalyiaa, and Hazelle would be watching the house for me. Even before I put one mile on the Hoka shoes I kept thinking about my granddaughter's. I kept thinking they don't have a clue regarding the journey upon which I'm about to embark. I also thought that they will be able to read about their retired grandfather in about 20 years making history while contributing services to those in need. I also had it in mind that my granddaughters will piggy-back off this Walkabout and do something great with their lives, because I know they will one day. As I was cruising down I-40 going East I was so fired up about this whole walking thing I found myself somehow talking to strangers at rest stops, and gas stations about what I was going to be doing. One guy gave me twenty dollars because he believed in me. I guess my enthusiasm was off the chart. I would have never thought that someone would give me money for just talking, but it happened.

> *"People, who are crazy enough to think they can change the world, are the ones who do."*
> *Steve Jobs*

"Man, it's a great day to be alive"

Dr. Kimbro once stated in his book, "Think and Grow Rich: A Black Choice," that *"Enthusiasm is emotion management. If you are able to transmit enthusiasm to others, you have the ability to control the emotional climate of any situation. When you can generate true enthusiasm, you can break the preoccupation of those around you, making others take notice and listen to your ideas. You can capture attention through enthusiasm and guide that attention in any direction you so choose."* I thought, WOW! This stranger told me to buy some breakfast on him with that $20.

That was a very kind thing for him to do. Enthusiasm is such a powerful tool. I had no idea this Walkabout-America deal would snowball into this huge success, and mainly it's due to being so enthusiastic. I had to be! I had to keep my mind stuck in the go forward position. "Perpetual motion moving forward." I would tell myself that over and over again with some enthusiasm mixed in. My truck "Wilbur" made it to the unbridled spirit state of Kentucky with no problem. Wilbur and I looked good as we crossed the state line. It seemed to me that the truck was all buffed up from the things that were bulging out of the back of bed. The Chuck Norris machine was one of the things it was carrying cross country. That's what I used to get buffed.

It was awesome seeing my mom and dad. I hadn't seen them for over a year and it felt good. I was already missing my grandbabies in Albuquerque. It was late March and Kentucky was getting hammered with rain and thunderstorms. Occasionally the sun would come out, but there were still times when winter would pop its ugly head out and dust us with the white stuff. This still felt really surreal to me, as though I was having a dream. But I knew it was real when I smelled my mama's cooking, her patented fried breakfast of potatoes, some sausages and eggs, with some hot rolls. On April 15, 2015 my mom and dad agreed to drive me to my starting point. The temperature in Kentucky that day was a comfortable 66 degrees. I was 13 days off of my original goal of walking on my birthday April 2nd. That's only because we had to push back the start date a couple of times due to the weather in New England. My mom and dad drove me up in their 36-foot recreation vehicle who we called, "Big Liz". The most memorable moment with Big Liz was when it was my turn to drive. I turned onto a road where Big Liz was not supposed to travel. She was too tall for the sides of the old archway viaduct, which meant I was having to drive right down the middle, taking up two lanes.

"Do what you have to do, to do what you want to do." Denzel Washington

"Man, it's a great day to be alive"

Each time I would burst through one of the old arched viaducts I would have to straddle Big Liz right in the middle of the two-lane road and block traffic from passing me so I could clear the archway. Invariably, the traffic in back of us would get mad. I would also cringe each time we would go cruising under one of the archways at 60mph thinking I would knock the air conditioner unit off the top of the vehicle. That was fun, but a little nerve wracking.

Somehow, we ended up driving through New Jersey. I thought they had the worst roads that I've ever experienced, right around the toll booth area. They had pot holes that would engulf and hide a small VW bug. Big Liz gracefully slammed down one tire after another, with it sounding like we'd just broken an axle. The toll was very expensive, and I asked myself where all that toll money was going, because these roads sucked! Hours later, we finally came upon a bridge where I could see the state line sign which was over a body of water, the Piscataqua River. We had at last reached our starting point state, Maine. Man, it felt like I was in the Olympics standing on the top of a downhill slalom course. I was looking down and listening to the timer beeping, counting down for me to shove off. First things first, we had to find a restaurant so we could experience fresh lobster from the Northeast.

We finally arrived in Portland, Maine. After helping Dad, as a ground guide for parking Big Liz, we finally squeezed her in beside one of the office buildings and found a restaurant. My dad and mom's eating habit was something I had to get used to. I felt like the Beverly Hillbillies, with me being Jethro, Mom being Granny, and Dad being Jed. I said to myself, "Patience, Grasshopper" everything in life is temporary. This moment will be over tonight and I will soon be in the presence of good old Mother

Nature. I will soon be longing for their old country ways after a few hundred miles down the road."

This was my first time visiting this state. I would always try to visualize what this state would look like from the magazines and the movies, it seemed exactly like what I pictured. We could see boats on the water and those long, floating dock walkways. The restaurant was like no other I had eaten at with my parents. The restaurant was in the confines of a boat, imagine that. LOL. The Beverly Hillbillies factor was in full effect. It was somewhat comical watching my parents acting as if they knew how to place the cloth napkin in their laps, or not trying, or trying, to talk with food in their mouth. I thought it was funny, and I love them dearly.

"Love one another as I have loved you." John 15:12

"Man, it's a great day to be alive"

Yes sir, this will all be over in a few days, and I'm looking forward to good old Mother Nature. We all decided on the restaurant and lounge called DiMillo's On The Water. The owner Johnny DiMillo gave me a free meal when he heard what I was doing and why I was doing it. Johnny gave me a handful of his restaurant's business cards so that I could write my website, my name and the Make-A-Wish foundation information on the back of them to hand out when people would ask how they could help the children. That was very nice of him to do.

That was my sign of the great "My Country Tis of Thee, Sweet Land of Liberty" hospitality. It gave me the feeling of joy to know that there are still good people in the world. My first day in Maine was a good day, thank God. Before this walk, I sat down for on average, three hours a day doing research on each state through which I was walking. Mainly to get some history on each state's gun laws and some Black history of each of the state's horrific acts dating back to 1959 (the year I was born), particularly the number of Blacks that were lynched in the states I would be traversing. I think what made me choose to conjure up this dark remembrance of our American history was the fact that I would be walking these lonely back roads. Some of these same lonely back roads where some of my ancestors could have been hung, because of the color of their skin. It blows my mind. It also blows my mind how injustice is still prevalent today (Black Lives Matter). Somehow, this research started an itch that ignited my curiosity about lynching's.

Did you know, *"In the South, people were blaming their financial problems on the newly freed slaves who lived around them. Lynching's were becoming a popular way of resolving some of the anger that whites had in relation to the*

free Blacks. From 1882-1968, 4,743 lynching's occurred in the United States."
(NAACP | History of Lynching's www.naacp.org/history-of-lynchings/)

This Walkabout-America made me also think of what my ancestors had to go through when they had to walk and didn't have a choice in the matter. Their walks were much more dangerous than my walk. As a matter of fact there's one individual who sticks in my mind like peanut butter on the roof of my mouth.

"The strongest factor for success is self-esteem: Believing you can do it, believing you desire it and believing you will get it." **Unknown**

"Man, it's a great day to be alive"

His name is George Washington Carver (Inventor, Educator, and Leader). I can remember walking in Missouri, with it raining sheets sideways, and the thunder clapping so loud it felt like that low muffled vibration that goes completely through your body. Like that car in back of you somewhere that's playing a low, loud, annoying thumping so-called music. It kind of vibrates through your entire body like the thunder was doing as I walked. Carver walked through a few states to get his education with the possibility of him being lynched. Thank God he didn't, and we are a better world for it. The research that I found regarding the state of Maine stated there were zero blacks lynched in 1959, but one white. Not all of the United States lynched Black people; Alaska, Rhode Island, New Hampshire, Massachusetts, and Connecticut were the few states that had no lynching's of whites or blacks between 1882-1968.

These were things that I thought about most days as I was walking. You have plenty of time to go over your thoughts, again and again.

Now we fast forward to 2015 during my Walkabout-America. I also did some research after the Walkabout-America, which was, "There were 120 unarmed Black Americans who died as a result of police shootings" in the 13 states I walked through (Black Lives Matter).These two devastating acts (why we were lynched and being murdered by police officers) are acts of fear. 2 Timothy 1:7 says; *"For God has not given us a spirit of fear, but of power and of love and of a sound mind."*

I find it mind-boggling, walking and not getting harmed in the least. I'm a Black man who wore my hoody in the same states those fellow Americans who died, wore theirs. I was transformed as a replica of the people who were shot, with my long white/gray beard and coco dark skin. I was stopped and questioned by police officers 21 times throughout the entire journey. I thought while walking, *What would it be like if I or we as a race class of people (Negro, Black, African-Americans, Black-American) had the privileges of a white person at the beginning of history and all-times in today's life.* For example, I can have on a nice, professional looking suit and tie, go into some high end stores in a major city, and I would still be followed as though I'm going to do some shoplifting. That's not cool.

"Man, it's a great day to be alive"

While working security with the Sears Corporation part-time in Albuquerque, I learned Loss Prevention (LP). With that experience I'm able to spot an LP employee a mile away. I had plenty of time to ponder these thoughts and many others while walking at 3mph . The Random House Dictionary (1993) defines privilege as "a right, immunity, or benefit enjoyed only by a person beyond the advantages of most." I say this because "when you have a lot of time to think, you think a lot of times." I thought about a lot of things. I thought about life, finances, relationship, music, history, family, retirement, housing, weather, traffic, wildlife, Facebook, police shootings, and my body just to name a few. With the two things like lynching's back in 1959 the year I was born, and Black-Lives Matter (Michael Brown, Tamir Rice, Freddie Gray, Eric Gardner, Trayvon Martin), with the police shootings in 2015 (particular focus on the 13 States I walked through), the year I walked, took forefront with my most critical thinking. I say again these things are very important to me as a person and it feels good being able to write openly on what I feel and not be persecuted, stoned, or imprisoned. I love America, and it is a great place to live. I learned as I was walking that our first president George Washington owned 11 slaves which he received on his 11th birthday from his father as a present. By the time of Washington's death in 1799 he owned 124 slaves, leased 40 slaves and controlled 153 dower slaves.

"Slavery and the Washington's; Number of enslaved Africans assigned to widow Martha Custis as part of the dower share of her late husband's estate. Because she does not own, but has a lifetime use of these enslaved Africans and of their increase (future children and grandchildren), they are called dower slaves." **USHistory.org>slaves>numbers**

I bring this up because I was taught from the American school system that our first president did all these great things, and we were never told of the not so great things he did (like owning another individual that was considered 3/5 human) with no regard for those unfortunates without the privileged life he had. I feel today in my life I am privileged more than others, and others are privileged more than me. I am reaping the benefit enjoyed beyond the advantages of most, and it's from the walk. I can remember a time during the walk when patience was ever so needed. One day I walked for about eight and a half hours to Tionesta, Pennsylvania. When I stopped for the day, it was dark. It's not cool setting up your campsite and eating in the dark. I did this three times during my entire walkabout, and with a calm state of mind it always worked out. The patience came as I was walking along Rt. 36 north to get to where I was headed for the day and I had an Amish standoff encounter.

"Man, it's a great day to be alive"

I could see way off in a distance the black silhouette image of a man, horse and buggy bobbing up and down with the rolling hills. They were heading towards me, or I was walking towards them. That day I chose to walk into the traffic, it seemed a little safer. Believe it or not on my lazy days walking I chose to walk into the traffic. It was less thinking or more or less calculated thinking, I don't really know for a fact. It just felt comfortable. With that I would like to reiterate what Shari Arison said; *"Doing Good is a simple and universal vision. A vision to which each and every one of us can connect and contribute to its realization. A vision based on the belief that by doing good deeds, positive thinking and affirmative choice of words, feelings and actions, we can enhance goodness in the world."*

I know this sound nuts, but when walking into the traffic I somehow reassured myself that if I could see the cars coming head-on I would be able to use my superhero strength and jump either over the top of the oncoming car, or either jump out of the way just in the nick of time, just like in the movies. This method worked the whole walk. When I walked with the traffic at my back I made faster times for the day. I could pump out 20 to 30 miles with no problem. And when I would get about 3 to 5 miles from entering the towns I was walking to, I would put on some Prince or Michael Jackson, and I would say "bring us home, Michael," or "bring us home, Prince." I would put the iPod on repeat and blast it while playing "Raspberry Beret" by Prince or "Black or White" by Michael Jackson. They were the only two songs I would use for this. I called this a fast-five walk. It's like getting to the finish line and pushing so hard at the end and not to let anyone catch and pass you right at the very end. I would use the term fast-five walk a lot during the trek. I used other artists' like Nickelback or some Notorious "BIG" Biggy Smalls when pushing up a steep hill, and I would play William Gutierrez' "Native Flutes" music or Rochester Symphony Orchestra's "Classical Music" when I could physically see 50 miles plus ahead of me. The other variables were the weather; it had to be in the comfortable 70s with very low wind speeds and a flat new road, which made the fast-five walk work possible. As the Amish gentleman and I started getting closer to one another I thought I'm going to play a game of chicken with him. Little did I know he was doing the same thing. We got closer and closer and over the next little hill he pops up. Now the great Walkabout-America face-off was here.

"The two most important days in your life are the day you are born, and the day you find out why." Mark Twain

"Man, it's a great day to be alive"

I know I was walking opposite traffic and was even thinking "maybe I should get over" and then I said to myself NO, me and Esmeralda are going to stand our ground and he will have to go around us. And besides, if he gets into the road going around me traffic will be at his back, I think it's much safer than me getting into the road facing oncoming traffic. So there we are standing in the road looking at each other. I erected myself up to stand at my full 6 foot 2 inch stature with my chest slightly bulged out and was trying to make eye contact with the man. It was a cool to cold wet drizzly day for the most part. I would catch myself laughing at times as we were at a stalemate on the side of the road. I was laughing at the horse as it started rearing up and twisting around. I could tell the horse was very uncomfortable. I was also laughing at the Amish gentleman because he had this leather type of material stretched across the front of his Amish open horse drawn buggy to act as a wind blocker as he rode in the buggy. The leather material wind blocker had two slits/cuts in it and he had both his hands through them holding on to the reins of the horse. And I could not see his mouth, because it was below the leather wind blocker. So when I looked up at him sitting there, all I could see were his eyes and that black Stetson Amish fur cowboy hat, it tickled me. LOL

I still laugh about it today when I think of that image. He finally went around me and I yelled out in a loud voice, "Thank You!" and he didn't acknowledge me, but I did hear him mumble something under his breath as he passed me. Maybe that was his restraint from giving me the finger sign, I don't know. And maybe standing still was my restraint to just laugh and not get angry. I thought this is something I don't see every day, and I'm sure he thought the same. With all this, the bottom line is that I used an extraordinary amount of patience in that one moment (standing still).

Sometimes standing still can be proven to be very powerful. It sounds simple, but people say this art of standing helps them relax, feel more confident and they are quicker to spot stress-related tensions that they can then clear. They also claim it has physical benefits. 'Standing meditation improves core strength, balance, bone density, power, awareness, sleep quality, body alignment, efficiency of movements, and mind-body connection,' says Yang.

It is also quoted, "*The more still you are on the outside the more movement can happen within. 'It's like taking a magnifying glass and watching movements in more detail in the body, so you notice where there is tension,'* says Karel Koskuba, co-author of "Tai Chi for Every Body".

"Man, it's a great day to be alive"

If you think about it, cavemen had to stand still for hours when hunting for food. The wild animals like the lions and tigers have to stand still to overpower their prey. While the domestic house cat archly strikes a pose and it stands still getting powerful. And we as human beings have to stand still to engage the power within to accomplish certain things. Like your mom's most powerful, attention grabbing mad dog stare down. Especially if you were out of reach from her. She would be standing very still and looking powerful with a tight snarl on her face and with those beaming eyes that go right through you. You knew without a shadow of a doubt her stillness meant business. What does a rattlesnake do when it is about to strike, they lay perfectly still and with precise accuracy they hit their target. I had some great conversation with Esmeralda. At her (Esmeralda) fullest girth she probably weighed in at 225 pounds. And that's no walk in the park when you're pushing her big heavy girth up those New England nooks about 7000ft. I can remember when I first started the walk in New England I would over dress. Some of the hills were so steep I couldn't even walk one mile per hour. I would say to myself as I was laboring up those exhausting hills, "perpetual motion moving forward." I would say this quite often during the walk. I could see the front wheel of Esmeralda making that repetitive agonizingly slow movement with a piece of tape stuck on the wheel. I would try to count the number of revolutions as the tape flapped with the tire as it rolled around, but I would always get distracted. As long as I could see that front wheel moving and never stopping, I knew I would get there. Going downhill with her was just as challenging, I had to make sure I didn't let her go. I was very interested in the route that Cihiwsky walked. His YouTube slide show was something I aspire to do. I watched his slide show and listened to his music over and over again and again.

It assured me somehow that I was going to walk almost the exact route he did, but in reverse order. I thought, he made it, and then I know I can make it too. I often tell people God has given us ALL the same mustard seed. Now it is up to us to place it in good soil, fertilize it, make sure it's getting the right amount of sunlight, give it water, and lastly, keep the weeds out of your garden. Cihiwsky started his walk in San Diego, California and ended his walk in the Portland, Maine area. I said to myself I would be starting in the Portland, Maine area and finishing in San Diego.

"It takes nothing to join a crowd. It takes everything to stand alone,"
Han Hansen

"Man, it's a great day to be alive"

All of the long distance walking men I have mentioned have great self-reliance, Nate Damm included, which measures volumes with me. People with self-reliance I think are achievers, movers and shakers, innovators and those with the courage and determination to have the insight to say yes I can. I have often said; *"If they can put a man on the moon, surely I can find a way and I'll fix it,"* whatever it might be.

Self-Reliance is our responsibility and we are accountable for what we do with our life! You must understand you will get exactly out of life what you put into it. You will reap tomorrow the mustard seed you have sown today. Those mustard seeds could be relationship, finances, job, trust, compassion, sympathy, giving, or empathy, you fill in the blank. And the harvest will be ten-fold, so if it's good you're going to get a lot, and if it's bad you're going to get a lot. While training with Esmeralda on some of the back country roads in Albuquerque I would always get a flat from these three-prong thorns (goat heads). I said to myself I do not want to be fixing flats while I'm walking across America. I went out and purchased this hard foam type inter tubing that would prevent you from having a flat, but I couldn't get them on the bike rims. My son Wynton and I tried numerous times and could not get them on. I finally gave up and went to seek outside help at a local bike shop. The moment I walked into the bike shop with that hard tube foaming the bike shop owner said, "Oh No, we don't touch those things" trying to put those on a bike tire rim we'd end up damaging the rim and have to buy a new rim for the customers. So we don't mess with those. I took the foam tubing back to the store and got my money back. I still had the dilemma of getting flats along the journey. Then I had a friend suggest that I put this silver/gray liquid stuff that a tire place in town uses. I tried it and it didn't work either. Those Southwest goat-head stickers will flatten a tire right now.

After a few attempts in finding a way to come up with something that would prevent me from having flats during my Walkabout, my son and I came up with wheelchair wheels. It was a genius (aha) moment, thank God for sons. I painted the wheels a highly visible yellow and red, and the frame was yellow also. People could see me a mile away, literally. One day in California a couple stopped me and asked if I was painting the lines in the road because of my highly bright colors. All these things I mentioned are manifestations of the work God has bestowed upon me. And with God's help we can do all things through Christ who strengthens me, (Philippians 4:13). This quote was my number one quote throughout my entire Walkabout.

"Man, it's a great day to be alive"

It gave me the inspiration to keep on keeping on. It also gave me the ability to stand confidently in the doorway of a hole in the wall tavern somewhere in Indiana when I entered. This scripture was indeed very powerful as well. I was able to speak with power in my voice when I had to enter places like that. With the confidence it gave me I was able to speak what was on my mind and keep it at a professional level. I have often been asked why I used the term Walkabout America. There's an old proverb that states; *"The longest journey starts with a single step."*

That saying is ever so true, with the historical walk I did from the Atlantic to the Pacific Ocean. I have always wanted to visit the land Down Under where the Walkabout term originated from. So I figured by me speaking of those things that are not, as though they were would bring them into existence. The Walkabout America term has been used 248 days minimum in all of year 2015. I strongly believe that from this action I will be able to live this dream within the next ten years.

I can see myself with a very beautiful, positive, and gentle, God spirited lady companion touring with me and living my life with me. After being married for 21 years you often ask yourself if it is still possible to have a loving and caring relationship. I am sticking with the magic formula that worked for me in the past. That is stepping out on Faith. I have the complete trust and confidence in all that I am doing to fulfill what's due me. I believe in God as my higher power and with that said He wants us to be extraordinary and not ordinary. There are millions living the life ordinary, and do not realize what they have been given. The Bible (John, 14:12) says, *"Even the least among you can do all that I have done, and even greater things."* A person who has attained prosperity in modern society does not always come naturally. It requires the conscious act of making practical and effective use of oneself in serving others. Serving others I think is part of the even greater things. God was healing the sick and raising the dead, and we being a part of God have the same power. I think we can heal the sick and raise the dead also. Metaphorically speaking we can raise those dead minds and bring them alive with new and better ideas. We have our minds and we have our freewill to make up our minds to be or do anything we want in life.

So what will it be for you? Dr. Dennis Kimbro writes in Think and Grow Rich: a Black Choice, "Every creation of man, whether it is good or bad, is created first in a pattern of thought. All ideas, plans, and purposes are created in thought. As men search all their lives for worldly riches, they fail to realize that "the source" of all they would desire is already within their reach and under their control, awaiting only their recognition and use. Your only requirement for a productive, fulfilled life lies within the storehouse of your mind, ***If you will change your thinking, you will change your life.***"

"Man, it's a great day to be alive"

This is just what the doctor ordered. Each time we make major decisions we are changing our thinking, which in return will change our lives. I have seen so many friends and family members deprive themselves of all the riches and fabulous way of life because of fear.

Marianne Williamson once said;

> *"Our deepest fear is not that we are inadequate. Our deepest fear is that we are powerful beyond measure. It is our light, not our darkness that most frightens us. We ask ourselves, 'who am I to be brilliant, gorgeous, talented, and fabulous?' Actually, who are you not to be? You are a child of God. You playing small does not serve the world. There is nothing enlightened about shrinking so that other people feel insecure around you. We are meant to shine as children do. We were born to make manifest the glory of God that is within us. It is not just in some of us; as we let our light shine, as we are liberated from our own fear, we unconsciously give other people permission to do the same. Our presence automatically liberates others."*

I thought about this quote many times as I ventured across the countryside. I could see and manifest the greatness that has been placed in my heart the whole trip. The manifestation of Godly presents played well for me in some situations during the journey. I was able to humble myself to make people not feel insecure around me. I also made many new friends.

Just like the Bible says in Proverbs 18:24 *"A man who has friends must himself be friendly, But there is a friend who sticks closer than a brother."*

I made a major decision to help others with the Walkabout-America 2015. By this I changed my way of thinking and it has changed my life drastically on the upside.

If you think about it; having great wealth is nothing but having great thoughts. The smaller your thoughts, the smaller your wealth, think about it.

Dr. Wayne Dyer once said, *"When you change the way you look at things, the things you look at change.*

I often wondered if that was an oxymoron. It is a great saying and I take it to heart, because it's absolutely true. This is what I think; "When you don't change the way you look at things, the things you look at don't change."

"Man, it's a great day to be alive"

The military was something that really benefited me, and all who were a part of my life then. I had a feeling of, I can do anything when I joined the Army, you know, "Be all that you can be," but I didn't know what to be. So I drank, smoked, and focused on self-important things, but today I can count it all joy, THANK GOD. I was not being all that I could be. I believe we're placed in situations during life to teach us something (whether good or bad).

If we had not gone through past situations we would not be as knowledgeable about a lot of things in life. What the military produced in me was, respect for all people, teamwork, a person of my word, and it gave me the esprit de corps to be connected with all veterans anywhere anytime. I use the military as an example because of all the mental and physical training I had to endure. I can remember many times pushing down on that red dirt at Ft. Benning, Georgia shouting out in a 4 count cadence or stoutly upright in the Front Leaning Rest Position. The times that I was doing all this I didn't understand why. The walkabout-America thirty eight years later is when I finally understood why. I am thankful for the 25 mile forced road marches, for the countless times breaking down and setting up the Tactical Operation Center (the TOC) in the woods, and the sleepless night maneuvers with only the moonlight and wild turkeys roosting in the trees scaring the crap out of us. I believe that God has placed in our lives the seed to persist in whatever is worthwhile having.

This is a priceless treasure that is profoundly used today as it was over seventy years ago when Calvin Coolidge wrote this:

> *"Nothing in the world takes the place of persistence. Talent will not; nothing is more common than unsuccessful men with talent. Genius will not; unrewarded genius is almost a proverb. Education will not; the world is full of educated derelicts. Persistence and determination alone are omnipotent."*

The responsibility of being the oldest sibling has always been something I cherish. I can tell from over the years that my actions were watched by the other siblings. From the times I used to make them sugar sandwiches as small children, to the time I left my house for Iraq.

"Man, it's a great day to be alive"

The Walkabout-America 2015 has been no different. I not only have my siblings watching but, all of the social media (Facebook) and folks from the 13 United States I crossed. My responsibility as God's dream team member is to serve and love.

Helping others is the fruit of God's roots in me. Serving others has never been in question more, than during my walk through the White Mountain Apache reservation in Arizona.

Persistency of purpose is power. That power kept me alive in the most trying time of my journey. This is the same power I called upon and used during those arduous times conquering an 8,620ft push up a canyon. It was Henry David Thoreau who wrote:

> *"If one advances confidently in the direction of his [or her]
> dreams and endeavors to live the life he [or she] has imagined,
> he [or she] will meet success unexpected in common hours."*

The factual quote of Thoreau is in the direct path of walking by Faith. I came to the realization that Faith works. I experienced GREAT things (over and over again) happening to me after some very HARD challenging issues on the journey.

I think I was in the first leg of the walk (in New England) when this manifestation from the divine supernatural accrued (epiphany). It's a little difficult to sum up in words when it comes to trying to explain. It's like you know you have a brain in your head. You know it works, because you use it every day. But can you see it? No you can't. You can see your brain, no more than you can see a thought. But in each situation you use both every day.

God has already given us this marvelous human wireless computer called the brain. In this book my job will be to help you tap into your inner potential and change potential power into real power – action. My reason for saying this is twofold. The first reason is you have as a human being, endorphins that will kick in from reading about some of the challenging things I endured when walking across America. Secondly is the reason WHY I decided to do this Walkabout America. In the hope of having the ability to identify with and understand somebody else's feelings or difficulties sprinkled with some sympathy/empathy is what my message is about. Each little town or big city I would visit I found myself being blissfully happy with the fact that I was helping someone to live a better quality of life. I also had time to think of how we as people think of self-first and others "maybe" second. Most times it would sadden me, because as a child growing up I was taught that separate was good.

"Take action! An inch of movement will bring you closer to your goals than a mile of intention." **Dr. Steve Maraboli**

"Man, it's a great day to be alive"

Beat the next guy, get the first place trophy. And not only beat them, but beat the snot out of them. Whether it's at a spelling bee, or beating someone playing football. Wow, I used to be that person. Now I have learned that I get the most gratitude out of life when I think others-first and myself a close second.

I have found that it is great when you talk about someone in a good way, and in doing so it never gets back to you on what the person might feel about what you have said. Now if you said something bad about someone to somebody else, it will get back to you faster than you can complete the sentence about the person you're talking about.

I'm not saying that doing something good for someone else deserves some type of acknowledgement (it would be great if we did, and it would be great if we didn't). Because if you expect it, it's for the wrong reasons that you are doing it. I'm just using the doing positive approach to someone versus doing negative to someone as my example. I think the world has taught us that bad and being separate is somehow good. Whatever happened to the golden rule? You know *"Do unto others as you would have them do unto you."* Everyone wants you to beat the next guy at their expense. Each one of the steps I took crossing this wonderful land from sea to shining sea brought me closer to others and myself (Anthony Lee Roddy). I walked by faith and not by sight. I have 3,073 miles and 8 months of hands on experience that worked for me. From the enthusiasm I used I was able to move forward with personal initiative and imagination. The courage alone with the degree of empathy kept me focused on understanding someone else's difficulties as I faced my own during the Walkabout.

W. Clement Stone once wrote:
"Whatever you can conceive and believe, you can achieve with PMA
(positive mental attitude),"

"Man, it's a great day to be alive"

Serotonin; The enzymes in your brain that make you feel good are considered a natural mood stabilizer. I read somewhere during a psychology class that the people who are recipients of an act of kindness, like someone who does something nice for them, gives them some money, or gives them a gift, tells them that you love them, hold their hand, and they feel good. From the small molecules in the urine, scientists have been able to measure amounts of serotonin in a person.

People who receive these acts of kindness have an increase in serotonin. Now get this, the study also shows that the person giving has a significant increase in serotonin as well. I find this astonishing, and another thing that's so amazing is the study measured the serotonin level in the person observing an act of kindness and their serotonin level spiked. I mention all this because during my historical Walkabout-America my serotonin level was off the chart. It's a feeling that is very hard to describe exactly, (being the giver) and it felt so good. Now the children and their families (the recipients) that I helped during the walk will also have that feeling that is hard to describe exactly, and it feels so good also. I noticed during the walkabout how people (the observer) would find out about what I was doing maybe from radio, TV, or the local paper and would make it their business to stop me and ask about what I was doing. And I would give them my standard saying; "I'm just walking, we do it every day." I can remember walking along the road one day and a lady was under the hair dryer in one of the houses and she came running out their woody type back yard in her apron. She was a petite, middle aged lady with these huge oversized hair rollers and that apron flapping in the wind like she was coming down a runway getting ready for flight.

She had just read about me in the papers and wanted to help by supporting the children. I will never forget that moment. Count it ALL joy. Walking across America takes all that God has given you. You must have a belief in yourself to know that we all have a speck of God in us. Besides, we are created in His likeness. God is love, and that's all we have to give away. I did encounter various acts of kindness in each town I stopped overnight in. Before I set out on the historical Walkabout-America one of my parents biggest concern was how would the police officers treat me along the route. It was something that was in the back of my mind also. Our nation had just and was going through all the police shootings of unarmed Black Americans men around the country. So it was a real concern for a lot of my relatives and friends.

"I think the whole world is dying to hear someone say; "I love you." I think that if I can leave the legacy of love and passion in the world, then I think I've done my job in a world that's getting colder and colder by the day". **Lionel Richie**

Chapter 1

Maine

MAINE,

"Man, it's a great day to be alive."

We arrived in the early afternoon around 2-2:30 p.m. and the weather was sunny and comfortable. My parents and I pulled into a rest stop to walk and stretched our legs. It felt great to finally be in the starting state for the walk. We continued on in search of a Wal-Mart to park Big Liz and put Esmeralda back together again like Humpty Dumpty.

That night I couldn't stop crying. My emotions had finally kicked in. I laid there thinking how sad it's going to be not seeing my loved ones for the better part of the year. I also thought how happy it's going to be not seeing them as well. But, yes there's a but, and a very big but, and that is I will miss my granddaughters every day. They are the exception to the rule. I could feel myself getting choked up. I tried to cry quietly, and I did, but the tears kept coming.

So, I got up and went to my parents' bedroom and we all prayed. It had decisively hit me like a ton of bricks with floodgates of tears non-stop. As I sat there praying and thinking, I knew that what I was about to do was epic. This large-scale effort would be my biggest individual servanthood to an organization ever. I knew by doing this Walkabout-America it would give me this feeling of total freedom, where I could do what I wanted to do every day. All my emotions were bundled, and arriving in Maine was like that needle used to stick a water balloon and the water just explodes.

The next morning, I got up about 5:00 am. and had my alarm set for 6:45am. I lay in bed thinking what to wear for the first leg of my trek across America. I refused to call my sister (Shawanna) because I knew I would have started to cry, so I didn't call her. Besides, Esmerelda was calling my name for me to put my hand all over her to tighten up her screws. Right now she has priority over any girl in my life at this time.

My parents finally got up and we ate some breakfast. My Uncle Joe and Aunt Emmer Tucker flew in from Illinois to see me off also. We all headed for Wells Beach, Maine for the big send off. As we cruised along the back roads to the beach I was looking out the front window and said to myself (silently) there's no shoulders to walk on. I was a little nervous knowing that this is it. This is it the Super Bowl of all walks. We made it and Dad pulled up with Big Liz in front of the merchant shop along the beach. My dad Clarence Roddy had entered the beach in a spectacular gala with his 36 footer RV. We couldn't go through the beach area because the size of Big Liz, so we parked in front of one of the shops that was opening up.

"Man, it's a great day to be alive"

The Roddy's had set up shop on a beachfront. I started unpacking all my gear and stocking Esmeralda with all the things we would need for the journey. There were a few passersby who asked what was going on. My mom started bragging on me doing the Walkabout-America and some lady gave her $20 to give me for the cause. My mom was so happy. After I finished packing Esmeralda, my dad and Uncle Joe walked down with me to the Atlantic Ocean so that I could take some pictures of my feet in the water. I had set a goal of walking an average of 20 miles a day to get to California.

Okay, the curtains were up, and it was show time. This is where the rubber meets the road. As I watched Dad, Mom, Uncle Joe, and Aunt Emmer drive away I whispered to Esmeralda (we got this) go west, by way of New Hampshire. Before getting to the starting point as we were driving, I would look out the window of the RV and say to myself I have to walk back down this road. And the road has no shoulders; I've got to walk in the road. I was a little intimidated and I was not going to say anything. As I walked the great "Dirigo" (Latin for "I Direct" or "I Lead") state of Maine it all seemed to feel so surreal. My emotions were running high and I had a fast pace. I had to get into a rhythm and I had not figured it out yet. It was too early in the game. I took a few pictures and the countryside seemed to be peaceful. I was happy. Yes! Esmeralda and I hit our very first goal. I was so proud of her, no mechanical hiccups, just a few blisters. We blew through Maine and reached Dover, New Hampshire 20 miles later.

Reaching my very first goal was monumental; it was like an adrenaline shot of Red Bull, I was pumped. Today was a great day. Thank God.

**"People with goals succeed because they know where
they are going....it's as simple as that."**
Earl Nightingale

<u>What I Learned in MAINE</u>

What I learned in Maine was to eat seafood with a bib
I learned to pack on the calories and not to tell a fib
What I learned is that people are people and they all live in a crib
Maine was a beautiful state, with woodlands
to the north and water to the east.

You can't go wrong with their kind of feast.
What I learned in Maine would change my life forever
Just like playing in the Far East sandbox
Which was not so clever

Maine was the starting block of a historical Walkabout
I learned to prioritize and make friends
Because the journey I was on seemed to never end
What I learned in Maine, from the pine tree state
Was to keep moving west and not get there too late.

Chapter 2

New Hampshire

NEW HAMPSHIRE

"Man, it's a great day to be alive"

When Esmeralda and I arrived in Dover, New Hampshire we got a room and we would dance our way through the entrance to get into the room. With me being new on this journey it was kind of like being on a honeymoon with Esmeralda. She was just too wide and too heavy to pick up and carry over the threshold. What I mean is I didn't know that all I needed to do is take out the most important items from Esmeralda and carry them to the room and lock her butt up outside the room, as opposed to putting Esmeralda in the room with me each time. By my first thousand miles the honeymoon was over and I would handcuff her to the rail outside the room each time. Now before putting Esmeralda in the room with me, I would have to take certain things off the top of her. I would then grab the front of her (6 foot body frame) and stand her on her hind legs to pivot walk her through the entrance. Each time I did this it felt like we were doing a 2 step dance where I would always have to lead. I had a blue plastic tarp that I covered Esmeralda with that kept my clothes dry from morning dew or rain. For all the times Esmeralda and I camped out, I made it a point to tuck her in.

The first hotel I stayed in (Days Inn) was managed by this young man young enough to be my son, and he was trying to flex his managerial muscle. I attempted to get some milk from him and he didn't want to give me any because it wasn't breakfast time. LOL. I then asked him for the corporate phone number and his attitude changed. The next morning, day two of the walkabout, I left the hotel around 12 noon and arrived in Raymond, New Hampshire about 7:45p.m. I got up the next morning (after having a great night sleep) to get myself together for the walk that day, and I needed some cardboard for the front of Esmerelda. It helped with the rain keeping things dry. I asked for the maintenance man; he came and he was very nice. He had just thrown some boxes away and I walked to the dumpster with him. We talked about what I was doing and he asked me where I was from. I told him a town south of Chicago called Joliet. He then said he knew where that place was, and my ears did a double take. He told me that he had some relatives that live there and one of them taught math in the 1970s. I think I remembered the name of the teacher, but math was NOT one of my favorite classes as a teenager. In fact, math was one of my favorite classes back then to ditch. I never got the whole math thing. I can do enough to budget my bills and not overspend. My favorite class was art back in the day and I can remember all the art teachers starting from the 8th grade.

"Man, it's a great day to be alive"

I thought to myself this was a very cool moment, I'm here in New Hampshire and talking to a person who has visited my hometown. The walk that day was very challenging. I was so far out of my comfort zone it didn't seem real. It started to rain just as I was leaving the hotel.

Now I'm thinking to myself this is going to be my first time figuring out where is the best place to put things like rain gear to be able to get to it fast before getting soaked. It rained all day long right into the night. Sometimes the rain looked like it was blowing sideways, and it was cold. This was my first time on the walkabout to use my waterproof gloves/ mittens, and they worked very well. The whole rain gear worked well. That road I walked (Rt. 155) had a couple of hills that seemed to keep going up, which was a task to complete. With my first day walking, the blisters on my feet were not so bad. But with me going into the second day, all day walking in the rain it caused discomfort. I found a Mom and Pop hotel with a screened in front where I could park Esmeralda, and get her out of the rain. I never realized how much water she drinks. And when it rains she gets heavier.

The hotel had a phone inside the enclosed screen walkway and a key box with the room keys in them. I had to call a number and the hotel owner answered and told me what key/room to take. All I had to do was leave my payment in the box.

I got out of the wet clothes and hung things all over the room with the heat blasting. My feet hurt, but I knew I couldn't stop walking for something so small. I'm walking tomorrow, perpetual motion, moving forward. Today was a good day. Thank God.

I can remember my first encounter with a police officer, it was in New Hampshire. It was the 2nd state (New Hampshire) that I had entered. The "Live Free or Die" state. I had done about nine hours that long day, and I was very hyped up, cold and wet on that April day. I had stopped at this gas station to use the washroom, buy something, and get directions. As I came out of the gas station I watched as two police officers circled Esmeralda like they were playing musical chairs. I then yelled out, "May I help you, officer," coming to Esmeralda's rescue.

One of the officers said, "Sir, someone called us and said you were walking in the road with traffic and had a baby in there (pointing at Esmeralda)."

"Man, it's a great day to be alive"

I said, "Frank (I could see his nametag), does it look like I have a baby in there? Come on, Frank, I'm bringing awareness to the Make a Wish Foundation for the children by walking across America."

He also realized what I was doing from the advertisement that my sister (Shawanna) had sown onto Esmeralda. I got some directions from him (Frank) just to get him engaged in a friendly conversation (I knew where I was going). I could feel from the conversation vibe, whether it was to be good or bad. And I couldn't help but notice the other police officer did not speak the whole time that we stood there. The other police officer had a bad vibe. I could feel Esmeralda slowly creeping closer to me as through she wanted me to protect her. I feel that if he would have been alone (police officer # two) things could have possibly been different.

He stood there with his arms folded and his tight sleeves rolled up on his muscular arms, like that police sergeant in "The Heat of the Night" (Alan Autry).

He had a big wad of chew nestled in the left side of his bottom lip and was trying to give me the mad dog stare down, but I didn't give a rat's turd at that point. I was cold and tired and was not breaking the law. I got some directions from him (Frank) and they finally left after running my driver's license.

Esmeralda and I couldn't wait for those jokers to leave so we could find a place to shack-up. I knew from the internet on my phone that there was one lodge in town to sleep at, but it was 2.5 miles in another direction off the scheduled walk. I then saw a gentleman wearing an Army cap pumping gas into a small pick-up truck. We caught eye contact and I walked over to ask him if he could give Esmeralda and I a ride to the lodge.

The man asked what I was doing and he noticed right away that I was a prior service member. I have noticed in my lifetime as a veteran that ALL service men and women have a certain esprit dé corps of unity "United we stand, divided we fall." He was elated that I was walking for the children and war veterans. He gave me a ride, and I knew for the first time on this walk, who I was and what I'm doing and stood for. The third day of the walk in New Hampshire was harder than the second.

"Perseverance and tact are the two most important qualities for the individual who wants to move ahead." ~Benjamin Disraeli~ Today was a good day, Thank God.

"Man, it's a great day to be alive"

I settled into the comfortable room after my cousin Nolen and his wife Pearl Roddy sponsored it for me. I thank God for placing the right people into my life to be a part of the mastermind alliance. Their job was to help me get across America (financially, inspirationally, spiritually, and social media).

I would also think of Dr. King and his dream; how he had a mastermind alliance that helped him accomplish some of the meaningful things he did, outside the box to help others. "I think we are placed on this earth to teach someone something, and get something from someone teaching us." Count it ALL joy. I can remember saying to myself, I've got to do a couple hundred days out here so you better get a rhythm, Tony. So start with sucking up any and ALL verbal comments on what I'm doing. I know exactly for a fact on why, what, where, and when I'm doing it. That's good enough for me and Esmeralda. She never complains about when and what and how I do it.

"Man, it's a great day to be alive"

Esmeralda had a rhythm; I just had to keep up with her, especially going down those steep rolling hills in the beautiful back country in New Hampshire. It rained a couple of hours in the morning starting off and then stopped. The sun came out which made it a very beautiful day and a real peaceful walk. After walking through the city of Manchester, New Hampshire I made it a point to talk to the Make-A-Wish foundation staff to let them know what I was doing. It was a great visit; I had a chance to take pictures with some very kind and motivating people there. I would end up staying in contact with them the entire Walkabout-America.

I could see the sheep in the meadows of the rolling hills. It was nice. The hardest part of this early walk was the rolling hills that seemed to never stop going up. I approached one hill and thought to myself, I have a strongman harness; I'll stop and put it on. I'm experimenting with it to see if it would be any easier pulling Esmeralda uphill. No it wasn't, and it was actually slower, trying to hook her up to the back of me (it was like trying to thread a needle in the dark). I was still attempting to find a rhythm. I was so glad I got conditioned for the physical part of the walk before I started. My plan was to camp out for the night, because I knew I had to doctor my right wet blistering foot. So I reached my destination and decided instead to rent a room and I got one. It was at the Fairfield Marriott in Hooksett, New Hampshire. The overnight stay was a clean and warm place to help my foot recover. I could see Esmeralda was digging it too. She was all sprawled out in her corner of the room with her flaps open (she was happy).

I needed to do a second day stay but I didn't have enough on my card. It was a few days before getting paid. I called my friend Lawrence Medina who was a part of my mastermind alliance and he sponsored me a second night at the place. My feet thanked him. I had a chance to rest and doctor my feet. Once I'm paid on the 1st on the month for my retirement I won't need the help with hotel stays. I kind of depleted my savings driving from New Mexico to Kentucky and to Maine feeding "Big Liz". But that's okay; I will be back on track next month, and that's in four days. Today was a good day, count it ALL joy.

"Life isn't about finding yourself, it's about creating yourself." George Bernard Shaw

"Man, today is a great day to be alive"

I got up the next morning, ate some free breakfast, and loaded up on some green tea bags for when Esmerelda and I are sleeping outside. Today our goal is to do a minimum of 22 miles and reach the town of Keene, New Hampshire. I once again encountered some nice hills but I knew that I had to conquer them to complete this walkabout. I can remember seeing this very large American flag (flapping ever so slowly because of its size) that made me very happy being an American. I then had a chance to walk by my first Wal-Mart on this quest. Esmeralda and I pushed across the parking lot like a snowbird's RV looking for a spot for the night. I located the almost perfect spot to lock down Ms. Esmeralda. I went inside and got some food for the night.

Once I reached Keene, I had to by-pass it to reach a place to stop for the day. During my hunt for a spot I encountered another monster hill that seemed to go up about a 1 ¼ mile while pushing Esmeralda's big heavy girth; it was a workout. I even had to stop and take a break before I got to the top. While stopped I would put together a powdered milk drink and eat a single serving of peanut butter to get some protein and a lift to get me over the hump. Once I reached the top I would throw my balled up tightened fist over my head and jump up and enthusiastically shout, "Yes," like the Rocky movie.

With me starting my walk late today it almost put my 7 hour goal for the day in the dark. I finally spotted a park where I could camp out. The park had a small brook that ran through it which I could hear running all-night. It was very peaceful. I got up the next morning and then again it was a very tranquil morning. I realized that all my electronics were dead. The prior day had no sunshine the entire day, so therefore my solar charger was not working. I had no juice. Today was the blueprint of yesterday with no sunshine. Wow, my first real physical dilemma on day eight. I believe in God as my higher power and I strongly believe the presence of the Godly laws helped me. For example, there were some park service workers that came out that morning to repair a wooden ramp at the main house. They told me that the park would be opening in May. I asked one of the guys if I could charge my phone and camera. He said no, there's no electricity on. There was one lady in the group and after that guy said that there was no electricity she boldly said there is electricity. She took my components and plugged them in for me. Thank God she had an empathic side. I went back to my camp-site and made myself two bags of oatmeal and a turkey sandwich. After a couple of hours I packed up Esmeralda and went up to get my phone and camera to hit the road. My goal today was to cross into Vermont. Today was a good day.

"Nothing builds self-esteem and self-confidence like accomplishments."----Thomas Carlyle.

<u>WHAT NEW HAMPSHIRE MEANS TO ME</u>

What New Hampshire means to me is 3,013 miles to San Diego

New Hampshire, New Hampshire your one of a kind

With your 14th president and Adam Sandler behind

New Hampshire, New Hampshire you're damp and cold

With winter almost over and springs will be gold

New Hampshire, New Hampshire this is a beautiful state

With the sheep grazing in the meadow, not a day late.

New Hampshire was hard, New Hampshire was great

New Hampshire was just another state

Chapter 3

Vermont

"Man, it's a great day to be alive"

VERMONT; "The Green Mountain State," when I think of this state I think of Aunt Jemima syrup. The welcome sign was a great pick-me upper on that gray gloomy day. I had a co-worker ask me before I walked, when I go through Vermont be sure to pick up some syrup. As I got a few more miles into the city of Brattleboro, it was rush hour. Nothing like the Dan Ryan expressway in Chicago, but nevertheless it was a rush hour. And wouldn't you know it, Esmeralda and I were the center of attraction. With all eyes right, upon Esmeralda and I, we stood tall. Like an old Army singing march cadence (standing talk and looking good, you ought to be in Hollywood). My goal today was to get to Brattleboro, before dark.

The day started off grey and you could see the rain coming in. As I walked along Rt. 9 west the skies gave way to some light sprinkles which gave me the opportunity to practice putting on my rain gear, and taking it off. I kept saying to myself that this highlander state will not let me leave until I've conquered another one of New Hampshire's strenuous hills. Sure enough there was one more hill before crossing into the "Green Mountain State" of Vermont. As I walked across the Seabee's bridge there on Rt. 9 all I could think about was I'm entering the third state of the journey, only 10 more states to go. To see the state signs when you are walking at 3mph gives you a whole different perspective on each state that you enter. I would always do a little motivational celebration. I would say, "YES, Esmeralda, we did it," (with a ton of enthusiasm) and then take a selfie of me and the state sign. The traffic was heavy and a couple of people honked their horns at me to either get off the road, or they were honking to acknowledge how beautiful Esmeralda and I looked together. Whatever the reason it didn't faze me one bit, I was focused. While walking towards downtown I could see that a police officer had someone pulled over. When I got closer the police officer, he just happened to turn around at the right moment as I was passing by him and the lady he had pulled over.

"You cannot do kindness too soon, for you never know how soon it will be too late."-------Ralph Waldo Emerson

"Man, it's a great day to be alive"

At that very moment he must have read the information on the front of my lovely Esmerelda and stuck out his hand for a handshake. I stuck out mine as well and it seemed as though he did not stop his conversation with the lady, and I didn't miss a stride. I thought that was a bit odd, but hey I'm walking across America. I found that to be one of the most peculiar things that happened in the state of Vermont (so far). As I walked closer to the downtown area I had to stop at a red light and could see another police officer who was walking the beat making his way over to us with undue speed. It was as though he wanted to catch me before the light changed. He asked me what I was doing. I told him I was walking across America for the Make-A-Wish foundation. The police officer (Matt) agreed to take a picture with Esmeralda and me after finding out what I was doing. Wow, my first two encounters with police offers in Vermont have out done New Hampshire police officers by far.

While entering Vermont, I could tell that they had a bunch of energy zapping hills also. I was pushing Esmerelda's big heavy girth up and down those hills. After leaving Brattleboro my body was exhausted and it was getting late. I had a young man pass by me jogging late afternoon. He could see that I was struggling with pushing Esmerelda and stopped to offer me some words of encouragement. He then asked me where I was going. I told him to California by way of Vermont. He said, "WOW," and started to laugh. He wished me good luck and continued jogging. I could tell he does this all the time. His body seemed to be in good shape. I noticed him running past me going the opposite direction. A little while later the jogger drove up in his car and got out and stopped me. He handed me a half dozen donuts and some milk. I thought to myself I'm in heaven and there is a God. It was just what the doctor ordered. I thanked him profusely and he could see how happy it made me. I found out it doesn't take much to make a person happy with small and simple gestures like milk and donuts. He then told me it was the least he could do. I waited until he drove off and scarfed them down like a wild dog on the African savanna. I walked a few more miles trying to figure out where would be a good place to camp for the night. The day was a little damp and I was tired. I had found that the state of Vermont had been the kindest so far. My perception was way off. I had never been to this state and I didn't know what to expect.

"Cynics will say there are no good people out there. And if you read the papers and watch TV news you could be convinced of that. But there are good people"--Jan Karon. Today was a good day, thank God.

"Man, it's a great day to be alive"

After finding a great place to camp on the side of the road it took some doing to haul Esmeralda's heavy girth up and down the side of a small hill. I decided not to walk the next day because of how the day started off with a great sunny morning. Besides, I needed to dry out and gave my body a good washing with the baby wipes, and shave some of the hair off my head. I could feel myself looking like a homeless person and sometimes smelling like one. But when you think about it, I was homeless. It took me a couple of states to finally realize this (being classified as a homeless person). It did not ever cross my mind before this Walkabout-America.

From the rain I was encountering the last 10 days or so, this sun felt good. I even had a chance to recharge my solar charger to keep me plugged into loved ones. With the truth being told, it felt good sometimes not to be connected to anyone or anything. The solitude moments I've had, would plug me into the Spirit of God's favor. And it felt great. So with me not walking this day, the morning started off very, very, peaceful and slow. I had a chance to read, eat a big breakfast, wash myself up, and do my journal. On that particular morning as I was finishing up reading I heard a big truck backing up with that distinct beeping sound. I got up to see what was going on, I could see down a small hill that leads to a small creek and a half a mile off this unpaved road with power lines. I finally crawled out of the tent and sat quietly as I watched this big orange truck beep its way back deeper into the wood line. Before it could come to a complete stop a man jumped out of one of the four doors. He had a roll of toilet paper (TP) in his hand as though he was running to the end zone with the TP flapping in the wind like the Star Spangled Banner. The man was shouting "I gotta go!" and he was headed my way. I could see the guys in the truck laughing uproariously at him. He finally lifted his head to find a good spot and he saw me sitting there looking at them. The man shouted back to the crew, "There's someone sitting up there." So he went into another direction and did the do. I went down to introduce myself to the crew members. They were all with a tree cutting service, there to clear the power lines that snaked up some of those New England hills. All this happened around 11:30 a.m. I met the supervisor and he told me that they were on lunch and needed a good spot to chill. The crew along with the supervisor wanted to know exactly what I was doing and one of the crew members noticed that I had on an Army hat and asked if I was prior service.

"Thank you is the best prayer that anyone could say. I say that one a lot. Thank you expresses extreme gratitude, humility, and understanding."---Alice Walker

"Man, it's a great day to be alive"

I said yes and then asked him the same question. He said yes and said he did his basic training at Ft. Leonard Wood (or Ft. Lost in the woods), MO. I smiled and replied with happiness, so did I back in 1977. I have noticed something that has benefited me so far on this journey and that is after spending years working closely with other soldiers you instinctively develop a bond of camaraderie.

I prayed to God one night that each person I come in contact with recognized that goodwill and lighthearted rapport within me that the Spirit of God has placed in me along with the military. They made a collective decision to not work anymore that day and have lunch with me and talk about my journey. They fed me cold-cuts, Gatorade, and beer, in exactly that order. After my 4th beer I was buzzing and having a great time with my new found friends. They packed up their equipment and pulled out of there around 4:30 p.m. but not without giving me some money, water, Gatorade, and beer. This was the highlight of my day. After they left I walked down to the creek to take a leak and sat down on a big rock pondering what had happened today. This was one of the better days on this 11 day walk so far.

"Man it's a great day to be alive"

As I slowly woke up I lay there and contemplated what I should do first to start the day. I must first figure out how to get out of the sleeping bag. What I mean is somehow I got turned around in the bag and the zipper is now under me, with me on my back. After mildly fricking out and twisting and turning like a giant caterpillar in some Godzilla movie I found the opening in the bag. The sleeping bag is military green and it put me in the mind of a juicy big plump green caterpillar that's woven itself into a cocoon. Then it was to find the old Gatorade bottle, so I can relieve myself. I know that once I'm 90 days or more into this journey I will have a system down and it will click like clockwork, even getting in and out of my sleeping bag.

"It is always a good day to be grateful for all of life - grateful for large blessings and small. Especially to be grateful for the symbolic blessings - the rainbows and butterflies that come into our lives when we least expect and most need them." - Jonathan Lockwood Huie. Today was a good day, thank God.

"Man, it's a great day to be alive"

I started my walk off going uphill, and by now I felt that my body had gotten used to the uphill push. My lovely Esmeralda was quiet for the most part as she enjoyed the beauty of Vermont at my expense. The weather in the highland elevation was still cool to cold. As I was making my way through the winding roads of Vermont I couldn't help but notice the maple trees with all the plastic tubing from one tree to another. A co-worker (Valerie Hood) who gave me my first donation for the Make-A-Wish kids told me before I took off on this quest to make sure you get some of Vermont's famous syrup. That saying played in my head over and over again as I stepped past all the maple tree farms alongside the road. I came upon this little candy/trinket shop off the road and I had to stop to get some of that famous Vermont syrup. Once I was inside the store I thought about bears and how they have a sweet tooth like me. They also have meat teeth like me, which are much larger than mine. And the only reason the bears crossed my mind was from some wooden carvings of bears in the store. So, after rationalizing to myself I got some hard maple candy I could pop in my mouth for quick energy while pushing Esmeralda up those New England hills, I pushed off heading west. The weather was a little cool but the sun was out and the natural features of a landscape appearance were especially picturesque. The roads were narrow and very trucky. Trucky is a word I came up with when I would count more big working trucks on the road than cars. These were construction trucks, some of the drivers were kind and some were not. I had one truck come past me so close that it blew my hat off my head. I thought to myself that jerk, he could have gotten over but he chose not to. On that note I had to relieve myself from the liquids I have drank. I pulled over, put a brake under Esmeralda's wheel and went down near the little creek that was running alongside the narrow road and did what I had to do. After pushing off again another police officer came up to me as I entered town and said that he had passed me about four hours ago and that I looked like I was on a mission. I told him what I was doing and he thanked me for doing such a great thing. The officer then handed me a bottle of water. He told me to be careful on these dangerous roads, there's a lot of big truck traffic here. I continued pushing and came to a supermarket. I locked down Esmeralda as people looked at me with that critical eye wondering, what the heck is he doing? Entering the store, I took a quick glance at myself in the glass and now I could see why people were gawking at me. I purchased some food and milk for my evening dinner. I had to be very careful of what I purchased because Esmeralda would get bloated and would snap up. The day was starting to smolder out like a match starving for oxygen. With it getting late, I started looking for a place to camp out. Besides, I had been walking for about eight hours or so and my body was saying rest me.

"Remember how far you've come, not how far you have to go. You are not where you want to but neither are you where you used to be." Rick Warren

"Man, it's a great day to be alive"

I was attempting to make it to Woodford State Park. I think the human body is magnificent. It heals itself, it tells you when you need to sleep, it tells you when to eat, it also tells you how far it will physically go. My body was saying please stop, but when that happens I just can't stop for the day. There are a few factors that have to take place. I need to stop at a place that has cover and concealment, a place that is not too far off the road, and a place that I can take a #2 (a dump) without anyone seeing me.

Woodford State Park was another two to three miles out so I'm not stopping. I figured that would be another two to three hours which would have taken me to darkness. I say this again, "God's Spirit was all over me and the journey." My mind was saying keep going, and my body was saying please stop. I really didn't know how far I could continue, so as I prayed to God to just give me enough strength to make it to the state park. I walked past this driveway just as this truck was pulling out to exit. So, I stopped to wave the driver through and give him the right of way; the man in the truck said, "TONY." I wondered who in the heaven knows my name in this little town. I answered yes (in a meekly not so sure way) and the man said, "It's me Matt, the police officer you met earlier, I'm not in uniform." He said that he told his wife about me and she wanted him to go find me and give me a plate of food she cooked, and now here I was walking right past their driveway! We stood and talked as the sun was fading ever so low on the horizon.

I couldn't stop smiling and saying to myself God is good. He knows exactly where He wants you to be placed. He also knows exactly who and when to place right people into your life. Matt asked me if I would like to stay with him and his wife for the night and I said no, I'm headed to the state park for the night. He then asked if he could give me a ride to the park.

I look at him and said that I'm walking and it wouldn't be right to say I walked across America and get a ride from you. He then looked at me and said the park is about 2 ½ miles down the road and it will be black dark in about one hour. Just deduct the miles from your total miles walked and don't steal my blessings I'm trying to give you. I agreed with him and we loaded Esmeralda into the back of his truck and he then took me to the state park. I couldn't help but to smell myself as I was riding and talking to Matt, and I emitted an offensive odor that my own mother wouldn't like. Matt never said anything about the smell as we arrived to the park. We exchanged phone numbers and to this day we still text each other. He helped me unload Esmeralda's big heavy wide girth and he drove off.

"The greatest gift of life is friendship, and I have received it," Hubert H. Humphrey

"Man, it's a great day to be alive"

The gates to the park were down and locked. I somehow scraped, pushed, and pulled Esmeralda's big girth under the gate and we were in. It was like I was entering an abandoned town with lots of tall trees. The sunset was falling like a duck landing, making its slow downward descent onto a pond. As I walked down the park's lonely road I saw a small house with a car parked in the driveway. I figured it was the park ranger's digs and I was right. I went up and knocked on the door and asked his permission to camp out for the night. He said yes and you have the whole park to yourself because the park doesn't open until next month. I couldn't wait to tell him I had just retired from the USDA Forest Service in Albuquerque, New Mexico. I told him and it seemed as though he really opened up about his job and told me the history of the park. He even mentioned that he knew a former co-worker I worked with when he called the Albuquerque service center. I then asked him if he had seen any bears at the park recently. He said no. But I knew he was shooting from the hip, just because he hadn't seen any, doesn't mean that there aren't any. I asked myself how could a place with this much wilderness not have any bears. I hung my food up anyway. I had to cut the conversation short because I wanted to set up camp before it got too dark to see. The park was beautiful. It still had some ice covering over the lake and a few snow mounds throughout, but beautiful just the same. I had a great night's sleep. So far I hadn't had a bad night sleeping since I started the walkabout. The park ranger (John) told me about some better spots on the other side of the park. There were lean-to sheds that provided a better cover for the night on the other side of the park. I took the day off and walked around the park just imagining what this place would be like on a hot summer day. I found a great spot to hunker down in. I set up camp and then ate dinner. I was sitting there texting a friend in Albuquerque, and just peacefully enjoying the beauty of nature when something caught my attention. No, it wasn't the squirrels frolicking around at lightning speed, and then hanging upside down vertical stuck to the tree as though they had Velcro on their feet. No, it wasn't the different birds flying and chirping but it was a dark silhouette of something moving around 75 yards or so out. I didn't think anything of it and dropped my head to respond to the text that just buzzed/vibrated in. And then as I lifted my head again I did a double take; at first I thought to myself someone's big black dog is loose. As I really focused in I noticed it was a black bear. It was going in the opposite direction of my camp, and it didn't see me. But nevertheless, it indeed was a black bear. This was something I hadn't ever experienced, EVER, a bear. The last black bear I saw was at the Brookfield Zoo in Chicago. My knee-jerk reaction was panic. I started thinking, *what do I do, what do I do*? Now this black bear that didn't see me probably would have continued on its way, but I had to do something.

"I would rather attempt something great and fail than attempt to do nothing and succeed." Robert Schuller

"Man, it's a great day to be alive"

What I learned from the military and the wildlife shows was to make yourself appear bigger and show the bear that you're not afraid (that's easier said than done). So, I grabbed my Forest Service whistle and blew it wanting the whole world to know. After blowing my very loud USDA Forest Service whistle loud as I could the bear stopped, stood up and looked in my direction. I then grabbed my bear spray and started running toward the bear shouting, "YO, BEAR, GET OUT OF HERE!" with me dramatically gesticulating frantically, with my arms over my head. It worked (hallelujah) because I didn't have a second plan. Esmeralda sat motionless, knowing she had all the goods. Then as I'm running behind this bear, I suddenly realized what I was doing and said to myself, *what in the HEAVEN's are you doing, Tony, don't chase bears*! I then went back to the campsite all nervous and shaky with my heart pounding 1,000 beats per minute. I kept asking myself, what do I do next, what do I do next? And then an "aha" moment (the light bulb went off), hang your food up, Tony, like in the wilderness shows. Then I started gathering my food and found a tree to hang it up in because I was thinking that the bear would be back. And then I thought, I've got to get a fire stared. That was easier said than done also, because there was still snow on the ground in some spots meaning the leaves were damp. The panic thing was starting to kick in once again, but I was not going to stop until I had a fire. The sun was starting to go down and all I could think of, was that bear is going to come back. After unsuccessfully trying to start the fire because everything on the ground was damp, I thought of my dry 54-page itinerary I typed alone with a sandwich bag of cotton balls and petroleum jelly mix. I started burning one page at a time of my itinerary until I got the fire blazing. Once the fire was started, now my itinerary that I was following started in Illinois and I'm in Vermont, I had burned 5 states of directions. That night I placed my tent inside the lean-to and slept with Esmeralda right at the front of my tent thinking she was going to protect me. The night was cold and I had the three sides and the overhead of the lean-to that shielded me, but the front was wide open. I didn't get a good night's sleep thinking that bear was coming back. The next morning I had a great hot breakfast before starting my trek West.

"When you find your path, you must not be afraid. You need to have sufficient courage to make mistakes. Disappointment, defeat, and despair are the tools God uses to show us the way." **- Paulo Coelho**

What Vermont means to me

Vermont, Vermont the Green Mountain state
You have to get up pretty early, not to be late
The birthplace of John Deere, with the colors of green and yellow
It makes me wonder if he was a good fellow
Vermont, Vermont with its maple trees abound
With plastic tubing that goes all around
You see the blue skies and breathe the fresh air
Thinking to myself, will I ever get there?
Vermont was nice, Vermont was kind
Vermont is a state that I will always have in mind

Chapter 4

New York

"Man, it's a great day to be alive"

Day 14 of the journey and it feels good getting close to the state line. My goal today is to walk for about eight hours and I will be in New York. The countryside was beautiful and I felt great, no aches or pains. After that eight-hour trek the day was coming to a close and it was getting late. I had to make it to the state line and then find a place to sleep. NEW YORK- finally I made it to that beautiful state sign that welcomed me to New York (The Empire State). The town was called Hoosick, New York. I did my usual when I reached the state line by holding up my arms with fists balled up and shouting YES! We did it, Esmerelda; she didn't get too excited but I was pumped. I would say to myself only nine more states and only 2,819 miles to go. I was in farm country and it was beautiful. I came up to this vacant restaurant with a dumpster out back that had a wooden six-foot dog ear fence around it. I said to myself almost perfect. Esmeralda and I snaked around to the back side of the dumpster area to camp. I thought it was a good spot considering it was getting dark, and there would be no traffic in and out of there. The building was closed and had a for sale sign in front of the yard. It had a marshy wetland in back of the property that was very active which held a frog orchestra that was awesome. It was a beautiful thing watching with excitement as the wildlife boomed. There were a lot of birds doing their mating calls and I could see this place was alive and this probably happens 24 hours a day. I was watching as the geese and ducks were kinda protecting their little space on the water. It was fantastic. After I finished dinner I sat in my small chair and watched the sunset as the frogs put on a performance of mating calls. The night was very loud but it was so cool. While I was sitting there a car pulled up to the front of the dumpster area and then another one pulled up shortly after. They could not see me and did not know Esmeralda and I were back there. The couple was young and they went into the inside of the dumpster area and started kissing and were about to make out but the guy didn't have any rubbers. The young lady kept saying (in a medium low whispering voice "you promised") it's not going to happen. The young man then said, "But I got this." I sat there a still as a newborn baby fawn. What the young man had was some marijuana. They smoked it and all the time I was praying that they wouldn't come around to the back of the dumpster and see me. They finally finished what they were doing and headed to a party they talked about. I thought to myself YES, only on a walkabout-America. Being only a little over two weeks into this historical journey the things that I have seen and experienced have been awesome. I know that as I walk through each state I am going to encounter new and more wonderful things, and I can't wait for it to happen. I am very, very happy I made this decision to walk.

"Man, it's a great day to be alive"

I got up the next morning and went through my routine of packing up Esmeralda, which on average was one hour minimum. I took off and walked around 7 ½ hours that day. I made it to Troy, New York, the hometown of Uncle Sam, you known the poster that was so popular during WW II. On the welcome sign there he was with that finger pointing at me. This particular day I thought of a hotel the whole walk. I had arrived in town, mid to late afternoon, and traffic was kind of thick. I got the usual stare down from the people passing by wondering what I was doing or judging me for what I was doing, either one I didn't really care. What I found amazing was some people who understood what I was doing would always give me money or food. I thought WOW, there are still good people in the world, and God is good ALL the time. I stopped to get my bearings and to look up a hotel in town. I can't imagine following a North Star as a navigating device like my ancestors did during their season as runaway escaped slaves. I found a hotel that was kind of on the high-end scale of things. I went inside to get a room and the desk clerk told me that they had no room at the Inn. I said to him, "Hey, what about a stable" like Mary and Jesus? We laughed a little bit thinking I could just go down the street and get another one, but the front desk person told me that there was a wedding in town for the night and I would be hard pressed to get a room. I didn't know what to do and it was getting late. I then thought of my cousin Dr. Arthur Parrot. I said to myself he has connections as a highly decorated mason in Chicago, surely he could help me, but it was a NO-GO. A big goose egg, as we said in the Army when we had to go through our Skill Qualification Test (SQT) and you didn't pass at a certain training task. It was the first time on the journey that I felt like quitting and saying the heck with all this walking, but I could see my granddaughter's face posted on Esmeralda and I said to myself, I've got to think. So I found another hotel across the interstate about four to five miles away in a town called Latham, and it was dark. I called a cab and told them that I had a cart with me that I was pushing and if they could bring a mini-van that would be great. It took them forever to get there, maybe because of all the wedding folks in town. Meanwhile, as I sat outside keeping Esmeralda company I saw this truck with Veteran license plates, I decided to camp out around it waiting for the driver to come out of the restaurant or the cab, whichever comes first. I figured one veteran would help another veteran for a good cause, and it was a truck with nothing in back. Esmeralda was even getting excited about it.

"Great works are performed, not by strength, but by perseverance." ---- Samuel Johnson

"Man, it's a great day to be alive"

The driver of the truck came out and I introduced myself and told him what I was doing and what had happened in the hotel (no vacancies because of the weddings in town). All I needed was a ride to another hotel down and across the interstate about three to four miles. With no hesitation, he said, "Absolutely not." I was blown away. I then said, "Come on, man, we are in Uncle Sam's hometown, surely you can help a fellow veteran out."

He again said, "No, I'm not going that way," and got in his truck and drove off. If I had some rotten tomatoes on me at the time or a brick I would have chucked it at his butt, so I just walked away. He probably thought I was this transient vagabond that was up to no good, and that I was making up the story about walking to help the Make-A-Wish children. I felt as though this guy was an impostor and didn't really do time in the Army. I am an American soldier, this is the creed I had to learn; *I am a warrior and a member of a team. I serve the people of the United States, and live the Army Values. I will always place the mission first. I will never accept defeat. I will never quit. I will never leave a fallen comrade. I am disciplined, physically and mentally tough, trained and proficient in my warrior tasks and drills. I always maintain my arms, my equipment and myself. I am an expert and I am a professional. I stand ready to deploy, engage, and destroy, the enemies of the United States of America in close combat. I am a guardian of freedom and the American way of life. I am an American Soldier.*

"Man, it's a great day to be alive"

This guy was a big NO-GO. The cab finally arrived and I greeted the gentleman who was driving and I found out from our conversation that he was also a veteran who had been to Iraq and Afghanistan. God knows why people are placed into your life and I thank God for not having that brick or rotten tomatoes near me to throw at that first guy as he drove away, otherwise I would have met a different set of people (the police). This cab driver was great. I could tell he was truly a real veteran with the Army creed in him. Our conversation went very smooth and comfortable. Richard was the driver's name. As we attempted to put Esmeralda in the back of the minivan cab she wouldn't fit all the way. We had to leave her front wheel hanging out the back and bungie cord her down like a car with an oversize piece of furniture in its trunk. She seemed a little upset as her wheel started to spin while cruising down the road. Richard told me which streets to take once I would leave the hotel to get back on Route 7 to avoid the interstate; he was truly a blessing. I told him about the so-called veteran that wouldn't help me, and I told him that I could have made it to this hotel here in Latham by walking around the interstate but it was dark. The neighborhood looked a little rough and I didn't want to fight anyone. He laughed and then dropped me off at the LaQuinta hotel. I had been conversing with the front desk person prior to arriving and they were very welcoming. The LaQuinta was clean and it felt like heaven after a long day of walking. I thought about that slogan and reworded it (for that guy that wouldn't help me) to say; "Uncle Sam DON'T want you." Yes! And with finger pointing.

"It is somehow painful when you can lay your life down for them, But they won't be there for you, Even when you need them the most." ~ Goals Rider It was a good day, count it ALL joy.

Anthony "Silverback" Roddy

"Man, it's a great day to be alive"

I checked into my room, ordered some lasagna, a small pizza and ate it like it was my last meal. I then took a much needed shower (with my clothes on first) shaved and attended to my blisters. I figured it out when it came to washing my clothes without a washer and dryer. I would shower with them on and get most of the day's salt off my clothes, and I would hang them up in the room (with heat blasting or fan) to dry out. That would get most of the funk off me but not all of it. With New York being my 4th state I was still placing Esmeralda in the room with me. I looked back on that and I didn't even give it a second thought of complaining about doing it, I felt as though it was part of what I had to do to complete my goal of walking across America. I find that amazing, "count it ALL joy".

"Life is good, I have no complaints." Barbara Robinson

"Man, it's a great day to be alive"

I got up the next day and decided I would stay another day because I needed to doctor my blisters, and do some journaling. It was a much needed rest and relaxation day. I spoke to a few of the housekeepers that were from Africa and it was a good day. As I was sitting in the breakfast area eating, the general manager came over to sit and talk with me. She seemed as though she was looking forward, eagerly, to an enjoyable conversation about the Walkabout-America. We talked for about an hour or so and it was a very comfortable and easy conversation. The next day after breakfast she wanted me to take a picture with her in front of the LaQuinta Hotel sign. She told me that she had arranged something with the corporate office for me to stay free at any LaQuinta throughout my journey across America. I then got my bearings and started walking WEST. It really felt good to know that there are still great people in America regardless of the color of their skin.

"Learn to be alone and to like it. There is nothing more freeing and empowering than learning to like your company." -Mandy Hale

"Man, it's a great day to be alive"

I feel good knowing I don't have to talk to anyone while I'm walking if I choose. I don't have to do face to face with anyone and talk, if I choose not to and that felt good. I don't have to pay any bills either, it's kinda like being deployed overseas. The real soldiers that have been deployed would understand what I'm talking about. It's a freedom you enjoy but it's for a limited time and then you come back to reality like a space shuttle landing in California. I often wonder if that same feeling of freedom ran through the soldiers' minds in WWI, WWII, and Vietnam. I can only guess that it was a spirit of freedom for the Negro soldiers in WWII, and Vietnam. I say that because the United States was not kind to my race.

So, with them being somewhere like France, Germany, or Korea, they had the freedom of not being beaten, hung, or shot for doing what all people do, living. I think that back then they had a feeling of accomplishment and they became heroes overseas. Then they come back to the United States, the country they fought so valiantly for to stay free, but only to get beaten, hung, and or shot, because of our ridiculous laws during that time. Wow, that blows my mind. It sounds like an oxymoron to me, either they would get cruel kindness or living death. As a kid, I would wonder sometimes if the words United States meant that all the white race of people were united in each state to do harm to the people of color. I know that sounds far out, but far out things did happen to me and my ancestors. I would like to thank God for changing the hearts of millions today to not do those far out things anymore.

"Time is very slow for those who wait. Very fast for those who are scared. Very long for those who lament. Very short for those who celebrate. But for those who love, time is eternal."~ William Shakespeare

"Man, it's a great day to be alive"

I only walked about 15 miles the day I left Troy, New York. I had a pretty good pace that day going down Rt. 7 to a town called Schenectady. It was a beautiful day, so I decided to unzip my pants legs off to enjoy the 86 degree weather. My goal for that day was to bust through that town and camp out somewhere in the countryside. New York has some very pretty countryside. That didn't happen because the route I was walking turned into an interstate. So, Esmeralda and I stopped and I had a little panic attack about walking on the freeway. I knew that it was illegal for me to walk on it from the sign I read.

I stood there for the longest time trying to figure out another route but I just couldn't. This caught me totally by surprise. I then turned around and started walking through neighborhoods following my compass west. I was lost in the hood, (sounds like a movie doesn't it) in a very heavily black populated area and believe it or not I felt a little intimidated. I could feel that I was the outsider. I could see families sitting on their porches watching Esmeralda and I roll through, and I had not a clue to where I was going. I would see drug dealers on the corner doing what they do, and they were watching me also. The area I was lost in didn't seem to have anywhere to sleep for the night. I didn't see any places to camp, other than in an alley or over someone's house. And at this point in the journey no, I'm good. I decided to take my chance on asking one of the pusher men on the corner to point me in the direction of a hotel. They did, but I count it all joy, with a little laughter when I get directions from some of these people. As I walked, I passed store after store and I noticed that they were all from East Indian descent. They were small corner stores and sometimes not a corner store, but they all seemed to have the same theme. To me it seemed like they all were selling cell phones, cell phone covers, cell phone

95

batteries, some foods, and a few other miscellaneous items. There were some Indian restaurants also.

"Too often, feeling intimidated becomes our excuse not to be awesome." ~ Scott Stratten

"Man, it's a great day to be alive"

When texting my son (Desmond) later I told him how I did not like walking through the cities. This area in particular kept taking me back to my childhood memories in Chicago. This was freaking me out. I lived in Chicago as a child during Dr. Martin Luther King's assassination. This neighborhood was somehow giving me flashbacks of the fear I had April 5, 1968 running home from school with my little sister (Shawanna) in tow. As the city descended into chaos all around us, this 9 year old and a 7 year old were making their way back home maybe seven blocks or so, I was scared. Man, which was crazy as I think back on it. I say crazy because as a 9 year old baby getting a 7 year old to and from school each day was nuts in itself. Now you throw in that the city is burning down and looting is all around with police presence, and I was afraid for me and my sister.

It's not that this neighborhood I was walking through frightened me, because of the Chicago childhood experiences, I have learned to adapt to any environment, I didn't want to. It takes too much energy to be negative and try to live like a thug wannabe. I had to switch my personality sociability to one that was harsh and pull out my street savvy card to deal with anyone who would approach me. It was hard enough trying to find a place to stay and get my bearings on how to get out of this place. I was now set back around two hours, walking around lost and it would be dark soon. I wasn't tracking with the directions I got from the drug dealers, so I stopped and asked a family that was just getting out of their car and they directed me to a hotel not far from where I was standing. This place was the only thing in the area, and it was weathered. The room cost me $60.00 and it had no cold water, I had to come to the front office to get a (one) cup of ice, and the room was nasty. I would have preferred to stay in the woods, but I was in a dirty city. The bed looked really, really, dirty. I did not want to lie down in it, so I pulled out my sleeping bag and put it on top of the bed and used it to sleep in. I ordered a pizza and some hot wings, went to the front office to get my 1-cup ration of ice, and went back to the room to watch the NBA playoffs. I didn't sleep well that night because of the constant traffic, all night long.

When you rise in the morning, give thanks for the light, for your life, for your strength. Give thanks for your food and for the joy of living. If you see no reason to give thanks, the fault lies in yourself," ~Tecumseh

"Man, it's a great day to be alive"

I woke up around 6:30 and made some oatmeal, and warmed up a slice of pizza from the night before and made some powdered mike with some cold water from Esmeralda and I was content. I hit the road about 9:00 and it felt great to leave that dirty hotel. I thanked God that I found this hotel and realized it could have been a lot worse. "Count it ALL joy," I could have been forced to bivouac behind one of the smelly dumpsters somewhere. Once I'd made it out of the ghetto and got back on track it was like walking in heaven. I had a really good feeling and I was very comfortable that day. I walked for almost 7.5 hours and was well into the countryside by now. Esmeralda and I had made good timing on the day's walk to Delanson, New York. I would usually under what I consider normal conditions start looking for a place to sleep for the night anywhere from 4:30 p.m. to 6:30 p.m. If there is no hotel in sight, I'm looking for the best cover and concealment on the side of the road, just a little trick I learned from the Army being an 11 Bravo infantry man. Who says you can't use your infantry skills in the civilian world. I agreed with myself before the start of this Walkabout-America to prevent confrontation at all cost. I agreed to do this not because I'm afraid of people, but because I'm afraid of what I might do to people if it came to that. When I would find a place alongside of the road that my spirit felt good with, I would quickly pull Esmeralda off the road. I would immediately pull off the orange flag from Esmeralda and right away take off my lime-yellow safety vest. I did that for the simple reason of not being detected by passing vehicles. Once I found my spot for the night, I pulled out my small axe and began doing some trail blazing. I thank God for giving me the knowledge to put wheelchair wheels on Esmeralda, because if not she would have had a lot of flats. As I finished setting up camp for the night I made some dinner (package of tuna on bread with a ton of mayo on it) and cup of hot tea, and just sitting there thinking of Bambi in the thicket playing with Thumper the rabbit. I felt so much more comfortable here than I did in that dirty city hotel. God had placed me in a good space today. It was great watching the sun set while I rest my legs and feet. I thanked God for placing me in the Army's Infantry. The Army taught me a lot in the days I was attempting to be all that I could be. I thanked God for giving me the strength and the fortitude to have the courage with the pains and adversities to keep on keeping on. Today was a good day, thank God.

"The world has enough beautiful mountains and meadows, spectacular skies and serene lakes. It has enough lush forests, flowered fields, and sandy beaches. It has plenty of stars and the promise of a new sunrise and sunset every day. What the world needs more of is people to appreciate and enjoy it." -Michael Josephson

"Man, it's a great day to be alive"

Day 17 of the journey. "Man, it's a great day to be alive." I walked for about 6.5 to 7 hours today making it to Cobleskill, New York. It was a beautiful spring day with the temperature in the 70s, and I had no life hiccups. Esmeralda and I proudly strutted through this town. It was a good walk. When I delivered mail for 15 years I would always love carrying mail when the temperature was in the mid-70s. I had the pleasure of walking past a gaggle of students walking from school. It appeared to me that they were High Schooler's, maybe around 9th or 10th grade.

I could see them from a distance as I walked on the opposite side of the street. I was walking with my back toward traffic as they were walking into traffic. They had to be about 150 to 200 yards in front of me. I would always make an attempt to catch a person that is walking in front of me by setting a landmark piece on side the road (driveway, mailbox, road sign, car, something) that I had to get to before they would. I did this for two reasons. My first reason would be to help me reach my daily walking goal faster and secondly the joy of accomplishing one small remarkable feat for that day (if I could catch them before they meet the mark).

I finally caught up to them (by the way, I reached the landmark first) and I shouted across the street telling them I'm walking to California, come join me. One of the students shouted back saying, "for real, hey, where did you start?" I enthusiastically shouted back saying, "Maineeeee," as I stretched the name of the state like a giant ball of silly putty. They all said simultaneously, "WOW!" And then one of the girls shouted, "Good luck, sir!" It was then I felt this great sense of worthiness, not as a Black man making history, however, but as a person doing something great for someone else. Seeing a mixed race of students walking who all thought I was a Wow for what I was doing, that really touched me. I kept that power speed stride with my head held high until I was out of sight of the town. I think the greatest enemy of mankind has been the misunderstanding of this thing called race. The people who I have encountered thus far have been kind to me. I made a promise to myself to only expect good during this "Walkabout-America".

"You get what you give" **Jennifer Lopez**

"Man, it's a great day to be alive"

I was now getting a little tired after seven hours of walking. I felt I needed some fuel for the day, so I started looking for a place to camp. Being at the outskirts of town was great. I was out of the town and going back into the lovely rural countryside. I spotted what looked like a plant nursery across the 4-lane road with a couple of people standing out front. The weather was good that day, and I thanked God for it. Esmeralda and I finally made our way across the not so busy four-lane road. We approached the gentleman that was standing there talking to a young lady getting into her car. I had noticed from across the street before crossing over, that the back of the nursery was on the side of the hill. It was overlooking this road/highway I was walking on; however, it would be a nice view (lookout point) from up there. It was away from the main road where no one could see me, but I could see them. (The old cover and concealment, courtesy of the Army). I then told the man what I was doing and asked if I could camp out on the hill out back. He said yes no problem. It sounds pretty cut and dry. Right? Just walk up to the spot and set up camp. Wrong. I started thinking it's not such a good sight as I pulled Esmerelda's big heavy girth, getting closer to it. It was on the side of a hill where pulling Esmeralda was a heavy task. Whenever I had to drag Esmeralda off the side of the road it can been very hard and strenuous, zapping what little energy I have from a long day's walk. However, the day was getting short and I just wanted to eat. As I got closer I noticed three or four deer scatter up the side of the hill like a California wildfire. After I got up to a decent spot on side of the hill, I was exhausted. I had to sit in my chair for about 15 minutes to muster up enough strength to set up camp and then eat. I had just burned calories I didn't think I had. The definition of grit applied and I used every bit of it. I finally recharged enough to set up camp and eat. After dinner, which was two mayo and tuna sandwiches, a can of Bush beans, three cream-filled chocolate things I ate as a child, and an empty Gatorade bottle of powdered milk. It was on point, and I enjoyed it as much as sitting in a 5-star restaurant. After I finished eating, I put a light jacket on and sat in my chair and looked out at Highway 88, watching and listening to the cars and trucks zoom by in the distance.

"Always give your all in everything you do because when you look back, you will know you gave your best with what you had and you will be so grateful for how far you have come." Melania Koulouris

"Man, it's a great day to be alive"

I finally made my way into my tent for the night. With the terrain on the little uneven side I had to make do with what I was dealt. Can you say exhausting, because that's how I felt after a so-called night's sleep. The hill I slept on had an incline that kept me sliding down in my sleeping bag all night. I fell asleep listening to the traffic pass in the distance. I would unconsciously pull myself up the entire night when I would feel myself sliding down. I woke up around 5:00 a.m. to relieve myself and fell back to sleep. I wouldn't dare get out of that nice warm tent to do a number 1. I did the first time I camped out on the journey, but two weeks or so into this now, the Gatorade bottle and I work almost perfectly together. It was a good fit (ya babe, me and my bottle). The bottle would fill up. Then I would unzip enough of the tent's entry door to slash and sling the Gatorade waste in front and toward the side of the tent. I would always sling it in a three in a three-motion movement. What I mean by that is like Zorro. Can you remember how he did the letter Z with his sword? It was from left to right, down and then right to left, and then left to right. That's the three-motion movement I was talking about. I then lay back down and fell into a deep, deep sleep only to be awakened by a semi-truck. That truck was using its Jake brake (gearing down of the motor) instead of his regular brakes to slow down that tractor trailer, and the motor startled me. With the unexpectedness of that sound, surprised as I was, I sat straight up and called out in a very loud voice "COME IN!" I thought someone was knocking. Then I realized what was going on and that I was dreaming about something. It was now even harder to fall back into that hard deep sleep that I was so much wanting back. As I lay there going in and out of sleeping I could hear the leaves around the tent shuffling and I didn't know what it was at first so I would shout out, "HEY!" to try to deter whatever was outside my tent. I then realized it was Mr. and Mrs. Squirrel. They were frolicking about without a care in the world. All I wanted to do is to get me a little bit more shut-eye before starting the day. One of these small bushy tail rodents decided to run across the bottom of my tent and it touched my feet. I again shouted out, "HEY, stay the heck off me!" So, I knew it was God telling me to get up and hit the road. I got up and had my morning burial and covered it with leaves. It was 7:30 a.m., an hour later than I would usually get up. It was a good peaceful morning thank God. I made some breakfast, packed up Esmeralda and headed west.

"With the new day comes new strength and new thoughts." Eleanor Roosevelt

"Man, it's a great day to be alive"

I got back on the main road and started towards Worcester, New York. This was only a 16 mile walk from Cobleskill, and I didn't hit my 20 to 25 mile goal for the day. However, that's quite alright "count it ALL joy." I have been using that quote I got from Joyce Meyers now for years, and it's still working "count it ALL joy." After I had around five hours of walking under my belt a gentleman by the name of Ron stopped. He pulled his car over after he had passed me and waited for me to catch up to him. Once I reached him the man approached me in a very gruff manner. It put me on the defensive right away when he said, "HEY, WHAT IS YOUR CAUSE?" as though I should not have had a cause. I also thought that was very brash/harsh. I said back in a loud and proud voice, "I'M WALKING TO CALIIFORNIA TO RAISE MONEY FOR MAKE-A-WISH!" He then in a much more civilized manner asked, "where did you start from?" I then said, "Portland, Maine." The man said, "I seen you about four hours ago and I had to find out where you were going." Ron said, "I think that's amazing and thank you for your service," after walking around Esmeralda (like an MP stopping you and spot checking your jeep on post) and reading the veteran stitching my sister had sown on. He went to his right shirt pocket and pulled out $15 and told me to buy some lunch, it's on me today. I said, "Hallelujah," thanked him and asked how far to the next town of Worcester. He said, "About five miles," and walked to his car and drove off. I waved at him as he vanished along the horizon. I finally made it to the town of Worcester, New York and pulled into a parking lot of Jack's Pub. I pushed Esmeralda up on the wooden sidewalk / porch and tied her down like I had a horse. There were three people sitting in the place. I asked the gentleman behind the bar if I could use the bathroom, he said yes, it's down there. I could see and smell that someone was cooking, so I asked the bartender if I could order something. He said sure. I ordered a large glass of milk, and a cheeseburger and fries. I then went to the bathroom. When I came out, much to my surprise a young man that was setting at the bar had paid for my lunch. He told me that I was an inspiration to him for what I was doing for the children of the Make-A-Wish foundation. I told him thank you and we exchanged contact information and we still keep in touch from time to time. "Count it ALL joy." I went back out to Esmeralda to get my phone charger to charge my phone as I sat and ate a high in protein sandwich and answered questions about the Walkabout-America with my newfound friends. Now get this, the blessings just keep rolling.

"When you focus on being a blessing, God makes sure that you are always blessed in abundance." Joel Osteen

"Man, it's a great day to be alive"

As I buttoned up Esmeralda's girdle (from getting the phone charger out) the two owners pulled up. They were a mother and daughter team (who owned the place) who looked as though they had been out grocery shopping. I held the door open for them. Once inside they listened while the men at the bar were explaining to them about what I had done and the purpose for doing it. One of the owners asked me how she could contribute to the Make-A-Wish foundation, and I gave her a card with my go fund me web address on it. She thanked me and said, "Now what do you need?"

I meekly said in a low and soft voice (as though I was taking her last), "Another glass of milk please." She said, "NO, that's not what I meant. I will give you another glass of milk, but what do you need to get down the road to your next destination?" I said, "Well, I could use a room for the night if there's a hotel in town." She went to the cash register and took out a $50 bill and gave it to me. Now this had been three blessings for me one right after another. I know that the Spirit of God has a great deal for all these things that are happening. I told her, "Thank you and may God continue to bless you and your family." I asked her how far the hotel would be from her place. She said about a mile to a mile and a half on this street. I finished my burger and my third tall cold glass of milk as she gave me directions to the Worcester Inn.

However, no sooner than I could swallow the last of my milk, one of the two gentlemen I'd met when arriving handed me a $10 bill and said keep me posted. He told me he would pass on my website to others. "God bless you, man." She then called the owner and when I got there, he (JB) told me he had a deal for me on the room. He then gave me keys and said we'll talk about it later. JB is an amazing man. He told me that it was an honor for him to have helped a war hero and an advocate who is helping the children of Make-A-Wish. The rooms were dated, however, they were clean and peaceful. The rooms at the hotel had no air conditioner just ceiling fan only, but that was quite alright with me. It was still early in this game where spring had just begun; the ceiling fans worked just fine for me, I was comfortable and tired. Jim also gave the kitchen orders to feed me what dinner that was prepared for the evening. While walking to the Worcester Inn not even a mile away, the walk was comfortable. Once I registered and got a room, JB was ever so kind. He offered me a spot around back where I could lock up Esmeralda, which I thought was great.

"One of the extraordinary things about humans events, is that the unthinkable becomes thinkable" **Salman Rushdie**

"Man, it's a great day to be alive"

While fitting Esmeralda in the back-storage area, Jim just happened to mention that the hotel has ghosts. I looked at him and said, "What you talking 'bout, Willis?" He looked back at me and chuckled, and then he told me that there's nothing to be afraid of. They are friendly ghosts like "Casper."

I asked JB, "Is this place haunted?" He started to tell me stories about some unusual and unsettling occurrences he had experienced at the hotel. I was a little concerned, but not deterred to stay. I thank God for a bold spirit to stay steadfast with the goals I have set to make it west. So what, it's a ghost spirit, I have God's Spirit, and it trumps the ghost spirit any time. I know if I face each day as it comes expecting that agape love that's in all of us, it will boomerang back around to me. With Jim telling the ghost stories, I was saying to myself God has not given me the spirit of fear (especially when having to get up in the middle of the night to use the bathroom). I have grown more competent, more confident with each passing day. So I prayed out loud in my room as much as I could and kept God in mind all night long. I slept wonderful that night at the hotel. There was no unusual or unsettling thing that happened.

At this point in the journey I'm realizing how incredibly nice the people have been in assisting me so far. The next day he and I talked about what motivated him to get into the hotel hospitality business. JB said he grew up as a dairy farmer with his father. He set a goal to do better than his father; he did not want to be a dairy farmer. He also at one time in his life was the youngest property owner in the state of New York at age 18. JB talked about how he did not agree with the Vietnam War that was taking place at the time. He spoke about how he didn't finish college because he knew if he did, he would get drafted as a second Lieutenant and get sent over to Vietnam. JB decided he would work his butt off to make a name for himself. In doing so he then could transition into the hotel hospitality business. Another thing that motivated him to do what he is doing is his belief in God. I could tell that he loved God from the empathy to understand the feelings that I had for helping the children of Make-A-Wish. Jim told me about a lady he knew whose son was granted a wish and that what I was doing is very commendable. I will never forget JB and his hotel staff.

"And then there is the most dangerous risk of all; the risk of spending your life not doing what you want, on the bet you can buy yourself the freedom to do it later" Randy Kominar

"Man, it's a great day to be alive"

I got up for the day around 7 a.m. after falling to sleep the night before watching the NBA playoffs. My goal for this wonderful day was to get closer to the state border crossing into Pennsylvania. My goal also was to be out of New York by Tuesday of next week. As Esmeralda and I pushed through the New York countryside it was a beautiful day. In the distances I could see something going on. There were cars and trucks parked along the road aligned with the white fencing that ran around the property. When I made it to the gathering, it was an equestrian horse riding contest for teenagers. I said to myself "WOW!" you don't see this in the hood. My mind immediately took me back to when Christopher Reeves (Superman) had his accident in 1995. However, Esmeralda and I rolled up like Queen Elizabeth in her 8 horse drawn golden state coach. And yes, everybody's eyes were on us. I walked with my head held high, as Esmeralda rolled along the driveway like a runway model in Paris. I parked Esmeralda and I mingled with the wannabe blue bloods there. I was telling my story to a couple of veterans and a family overheard where I had started my journey. Which was Portland, Maine/Wells Beach, Maine and we struck up a conversation. That family later on in the journey gave a nice donation to my cause (Make-A-Wish Foundation). This day had placed me in a nice spot in my life, and it felt good. The things and people I had seen and spoken to had been great with a capital G.

After meeting a few more families, getting a bite to eat, and taking some photos with the people that weren't afraid of me, Esmeralda and I continued walking. I walked to a town called Oneonta, New York. There I stopped at a VFW lodge that was opened. It was a beautiful and welcoming sight. Making it to the VFW lodge gave me a sense of comfort. I would always associate that feeling with an experience I would have when, in the Army.

I used to travel to a different post for training of some kind. It felt good to be away from your mainstay for a few weeks and share your camaraderie with other soldiers.

There was a man that came past me riding a bike who I spoke to for a while before he pedaled off. He was a very nice man. I often wonder if people who exercise actually stay happier. I know that there is a feel good residual that you get from exercise. I went into the lodge and introduced myself and told the four people that were there what I was doing. They welcomed me and told me I could set up camp underneath their raised patio out back. It was an almost perfect location with overhead cover and they left the door open for me to use the bathroom inside if I wanted to. I drank three tall glasses of cold milk and it felt like heaven with each cool gulp going down. The bartender was very nice. She brought me out a big pitcher of ice, and another cold glass of milk.

"Some people arrive and make such a beautiful impact on your life, you can barely remember what life was like without them." Anna Taylor

"Man, it's a great day to be alive"

She told me that in the morning there would be breakfast upstairs for a biker's club that would "love to have you there for the guest of honor." I said, "Really!" She said, "Yes, I've already spoken to them." She left and I finished off my glass of milk and called it a night. I slept really well and got up around 7 a.m. and went upstairs for breakfast. It was now Mother's Day. I will give my mom a call tonight before I fall asleep. I walked from table to table introducing myself and thanking them for allowing me to hang out. I also went to the kitchen to say hello and wish the moms in there Happy Mother's Day. The breakfast started around 8:30 and they introduced me as an honored guest so I had to go through the chow line first. I would have never thought I would have met such a great group of people (veterans) before I started this journey. I would almost always think about Mr. Willie Clay and what he had to endure when he did the Big Walk back in 1960. I had freedom; he didn't in the 55 year differences. I walked some back roads that gave me the creeps. I can't imagine what those roads were like in the 50s/60s. On that note I salute Mr. Clay again, because he did it. Today was a good day.

"Man, it's a great day to be alive"

I had to doctor on my right foot where a blister had formed, before I got started today. I walked for about eight hours today. My right foot had been giving me problems ever since my second day walking in the rain in New Hampshire. I started off the walk today in a little discomfort from that right foot. I knew if I would just keep walking that pain would subside, and the mind would wander off to another ache on the body. What I have learned from the Walkabout-America is that it's 99.9% mental. As I reached the six-hour mark of today's walk I could feel my right foot experience a really bad painful tear on the bottom. I didn't stop until I hit that Woooo moment. I think the blister busted on the bottom. I thought I could stop and attempt to patch it up, but when I stop other things are going to start to hurt, so I continued on to hit my 8hr. goal. The road I was walking slightly curved and sloped to the right onto a shoulder. I had to walk with my right foot uncomfortably sloped for a couple of miles which made my ankle swell up (that salty Spam I've been eating didn't help matters either), on top of the blister that just burst. I might as well be on the side of one of the precipices somewhere in the Himalaya Mountains walking. "I hurt" and it hurt bad. Today was my first day I really walked in pain. Man, let me tell you, I had to listen to some classical music to keep my mind in a zone to walk through the pain. I could recognize that I had the pain and I knew, once I stopped for the day, I would doctor it. I finally made it to Sidney, New York and it was dusk. I unplugged my music from my ears and turned on my GPS to locate a VFW or Foreign Legion. I was starting to feel a little flight or fight being in a new neighborhood and thinking that I was going to be walking in total darkness.

"It will hurt, it will take time, it will require dedication, it will require will power, you will need to make healthy decisions, it requires sacrifice, you will need to push your body to the max, there will be temptation, but, I promise you, when you reach your goal, it's worth it."-----picturequotes.com

"Man, it's a great day to be alive"

Walking in total darkness is something that I had not thought about doing. It's dangerous enough walking these roads in the daytime. So again, I salute Mr. Clay and his accomplishments (The Big Walk) back in 1960, where most of his journeys were in the night's black moon darkness. Thank God for technology because I made it to the Foreign Legion in Sidney, just before it got black dark. They were kind enough to let me in and feed me. They also allowed me to pitch my tent up in back, never mind that loud ground shaking train less than two blocks away going through town. After getting set up for the night I went back into the lodge to get what I had ordered for a meal and someone had paid for the meal. God is good all the time. I often thought about race, nationality, and ethnicity of people as I walked (besides, when walking all you have time for is to think). What I mean is, I would sometimes think like, some of the same people that treated me well are descendants of families from the 1950s and 1960s that treated Mr. Clay wrong and unfair when he walked across America in the 1960s. So, what has changed? This is a question we all should ask ourselves. I think it's a combination of what Dr. Martin Luther King did, technology, and the ability to finally exercise the 1st amendment (Freedom of Speech) with the strong belief in God. The Spirit of God is love, and love conquers all. I say this because there are more people on this planet today than there were 55 years ago when Mr. Clay did his thing. With that said, the more people that have a harmonious good belief can change and or shift the way of life to the better, most times. I was a part of that better most times. The people treated me with extreme generosity, kindness and support from Maine to California. But along the journey (the 13 states I walked through) there were unarmed people of my color (black, brown, African American) being killed by police officers. That in the very year (2015) and states I walked through. They were the not so fortunate ones, (God rest their souls) and that's what I mean by most times the harmonious belief works. I think this whole heartedly that, people who believe in the power of God, have that same power and can change things for the better. I would like to say, may the Spirit of God continuously bless ALL the families that were affected by the insensible killings of 2015.

"Everything is connected. There is no such thing as a coincidence, so trust that you are where you need to be."----Vybe Source

"Man, it's a great day to be alive"

Today was a no walk day. I needed to give my right foot a day off. I just figured if I could rest for an entire day, it would help with the healing process. It will also help me make my push closer to the Pennsylvania border. I did some journaling and listened to the train as it passed on schedule during that day. I met an Army airborne Ranger (Dale) who was stationed in Alaska when he served and seemed to be very kind. He must have bought me at least six drinks that night as I enjoyed the company of him and other service members. After we swapped one last Army story I told him I had to turn in for the night to get some rest. He said okay, and then asked me, "How do you eat your grits?" I said in a loud beer buzz voice, "with sugar and butter. Why?" He answered, "I will bring you some in the morning for breakfast, if you like." I said thanks, but deep down I knew he was drunk, and how many times have people said things when they have had a few drinks under their belt and it never materializes. I thought it was that alcohol promise you get when you're at the bar.

The next morning I was awakened by the sound of the mighty old freight train that snorted and sounded its loud horn. I got up and was getting ready to prepare breakfast for the day when the Ranger pulls up. He had the cheesy grits he promised along with bacon, eggs over easy, and this giant freshly baked biscuit, with jelly. I was blown away by this man's generous hospitality. He looked at me and said, "You didn't think I was coming did you?" I looked at him, smiled and saluted him. Then I shook his hand and thanked him for being a man of his word. He drove off and I ripped open a package of powdered milk and drank it with my hearty breakfast. It was like eating at the Cracker Barrel. It was delicious. God is good ALL the time. The night before, I talked to the bartender about bringing me some used panty hose that I would cut and wear for the prevention of blisters before I started my walk. So, shortly after the Ranger pulled off, she drove up.

"People with good intentions make promises. People with good character keep them." Unknown

"A true lady doesn't demand, she thanks, and a true man doesn't promise, he commits." Unknown

"Man, it's a great day to be alive"

She made my day all over again. We spoke for a little while before she then left and told me she had to come back to the lodge later to work. I thanked her for her generosity by going out of her way to the dollar store to accommodate me. She said, "No worries, I'm here to take care of the Vets. I will always thank you guys for protecting our rights here in America." Wow, I thank God for placing me where He wanted me to be on that day of my life. The Spirit of God has placed so many good, kind hearted people in my life; I wouldn't have ever imagined I would meet. And this is happening because I'm walking by faith not by sight. The panty hose trick was something I learned while doing 25 miles road marches back at Ft. Ord, California.

The next morning, I walked to a town in New York called Greene. I walked 7 hours and 14 minutes about 21 miles that day. It had been raining on and off the entire walk, which made the temperature drop. My foot was doing a lot better today than it was a couple days ago. I found a place off the side of the road to set up camp. I noticed that I couldn't get my hands warm; however, the rest of my body was comfortably warm. I thought that was a little odd but not a big concern. I pulled out my handy dandy flat small stove and warmed me up some soup. As I sat there sippy slurping out of a very hot metal camping cup, I thought of my mom. Because when the steam would hit my face from the metal cup, it reminded me of lifting the lid of a pot on the stove in Mom's kitchen. After eating the soup and warming up my hands by holding the bowl, this gave me some much-needed protein. This was also my twenty-third day of the journey and I had walked three states and was about to enter the fourth one (Pennsylvania). I was feeling pretty good about my accomplishments so far, and giving God the credit for bringing me this far. I finally got into the tent and let family members know that I was doing well today and in a safe spot. Today was a good day, thank God.

"Man, it's a great day to be alive"

I was awakened by the sound of trumpeting geese flying overhead, like a squadron of B52 bombers. I also heard the sweet sound of rain lightly pounding the tent. It was around 7 a.m. as I wiggled like a worm on a hook wondering whether or not I should get up out of the tent. I made a command decision to just unzip, roll over and used the Gatorade bottle. That was much easier and faster. I zipped back up in that fart sack and from the sound of the falling rain mixed with the early cold spring morning, I fell back asleep.

I had gotten really comfortable after emptying my bladder and was in that warm sleeping bag where I had fallen back into a deep sleep. I woke back up around 9:15 a.m., and the rain had stopped. I was way off my morning schedule of leaving by 10 a.m. but I thought that's okay. I made a promise to myself before the Walkabout that I would always, always readjust my goals for the day as long as I reset them to move perpetually forward and to the West. My feet felt great, I had no pain or blisters today, the cut nylon panty hose worked. I walked for 8 hours and 26 minutes or 24.7 miles this particular day to hit my mileage goal for the day. I did this in my hiking boots for the first time this journey.

"Man, it's a great day to be alive"

I started the next day off with the boots again, don't ask me why, but I did. I can see from the route that I had to conquer a few more elevated hills today. No worries, Esmeralda and I got this, besides I've graduated Hill Walking 101 from the lovely "Green Mountain State" of Vermont. The biggest issue when going up all these strenuous hills was going down them. I say that because it was no fun trying to hold on to Esmeralda's big girth attempting to escape so she wouldn't run downhill into someone's car. The boots didn't have the supportive bounce and for the first time on the trek I could feel a little discomfort in my left surgical knee. It kept making this popping sound. I kept saying to myself that I'm too far into this journey to stop or turn back now. I could feel my surgical knee starting to hurt a little more. During the pain in my knee as I would put on the miles I would say to myself "it's 99% mental," meaning I was attempting to block it out by putting my mind on something else. But I have to be honest, the first thought was oh poor me, I had knee surgery back in 1995, will I be able to finish the walk. That thought lasted for a millisecond.

"Even though all these obstacles keep coming at you, you just have to keep going through them. Because it's worth it to do something in your life, as opposed to fantasizing about doing something." Diane Keaton

"Man, it's a great day to be alive"

I then would always replace that negative thought with thoughts of my ancestors and what they had to go through back when they would walk in pain. This always motivated me to keep pushing west, and saying "there's worse things in life," *"I can do all thing through Christ who strengthens me"* Philippians 4:13. This worked every time, but I also had time to think of ways to correct any type of problem that would come up whether mental or physical.

This particular day, I remember when a semi-trailer truck whizzed passed me, and it seemed to sucked me down the road an additional 10 feet. I made it to camp after eight hours of walking. I found a spot tucked away about midpoint up this monster hill I was walking up. The area was very secluded and private. I quickly dragged Esmeralda off the road and into the bush. I took out my bear spray and the police baton to walk the area to find the best spot to pitch my tent, and to see if there were residences back there. It was all good (okay). I set up camp and ate as the sun went down along with the temperature. I turned in for the night only to be awakened by a pack of coyotes howling. The pack wasn't very far and those howls were creepy. I could feel that the coyotes were too close for comfort, because I could hear movement on one side of my tent. Then I could hear that same rustling noise on the other side of my tent. They were going back and forth around my camp. I would make deep loud grunting noises as though I was clearing my throat to let them know I was in the tent. I think the food I had in Esmeralda attracted them. I finally fell back to sleep with the comfort of knowing I had protection if needed. Today was a good day.

"To all general purpose we have uniformly been one people, each individual citizen everywhere enjoying the same national right, privileges, and protection."
Alexander Hamilton

"Man, it a great day to be alive"

The next morning, I unquestionably decided to wear my soft sole Honka shoes to see if it made a difference with my knee. If so, going downhill would be tolerable. I started the day pushing up a hill. Each time I'd begin the incline I would automatically think, *you can't go downhill until you go up hill. You can't go uphill until you go downhill.* With me doing that it did make a difference at the end of the day. I walked for about 7 hours along with 22 miles that day. It was a medium grey day, weather wise as Esmeralda and I arrived in Oswego, New York. There was a motel off of Route 17C which was perfectly located on the right side of the street at a decent price. Whenever I had to purchase or do something it was always easier to do it if the establishment was on the side of the road I was on. That day I was walking with the traffic. It wasn't the fanciest but it worked, besides I could see rain coming from a distance. As I pulled into the parking lot of the motel there were two ladies walking around the lot for exercise. They were mother and daughter, the owners. I stopped them to make small talk and that I would like to get a room. The mother told me to go down to the office and ring the bell to check in. I did but no one came. I waited for mother and daughter to make a lap back around so I could tell her. She stopped walking and checked me in. I don't think she realized that her husband was out walking the school's track down the street. I saw him as I walked by the tracks and waved, not knowing he was one of the owners. After I checked in and went back outside there was Esmeralda stealing, the spotlight again. This gentleman that I saw at the track was slowly circling Esmeralda like an art piece in France. I said, "Hey, I just saw you walking down the street," and he said yes. He asked me if I was a veteran and if I had been to Iraq? I told him yes and that I'm walking across America raising money for the Make-A-Wish foundation. He asked me where I started and where was I going? I told him and he lifted his right hand with index finger pointing to the sky saying, "Just a moment." He walked away and came back outside with a $20 bill. He said, "Here, this is for your cause." I thanked him and as I was walking away he said, "Those are nice shoes, and they look comfortable." I thanked him again and said, "Yes, they are very comfortable." I made it down to the room and unloaded Esmeralda. Then I took the lead and slow danced with Esmeralda to get her through the entrance to the room. Today was a good day, thank God.

"Kindness is the language which the deaf can hear and the blind can see."
Mark Twain

"Man, it's a great day to be alive"

I woke up around 3 a.m. and couldn't go back to sleep. I don't know if I was too comfortable, or just missing the dirty comfort of the campsite sleeping bag. I hadn't been in a bed with a mattress in about eight days. While lying in bed wide awake I started thinking how I could use this time of the day productively. I got up and made myself a cup of tea, wrote down some items I needed from the grocery store, pulled out my map to go over the route for today, and did some journaling. I could see from the map that I would be crossing into Pennsylvania (the state of independence) today, thank God. I walked for about seven hours with a large portion of that day in a heavy downpour of rain. Auf Wiedersehen, New York.

<u>What New York Means To Me</u>
New York, New York, the Empire State
With rolling hills and pastures you cannot escape
The city may be grand,
With King Kong at hand
But the countryside is mellow
To soothe all of God's fellows
With skies blue and the clouds white
New York is a state I checked off my list,
And don't have to fight.

Chapter 5

Pennsylvania

I made it to the Pennsylvania border and it stopped raining. I positioned Esmeralda on her good side to strike a pose with me beside the welcome sign. I did my routine celebration with a loud YES! And with fist clinched over my head with excitement I felt like Muhammad Ali standing over Sonny Liston. We took a few selfies and I started walking not knowing what to expect. What I mean by that is how well the locals are going to treat me. This grey/white bearded man pushing Esmeralda, who was over the top flamboyantly colored. Sometimes as I would walk down Main Street I could feel people looking out at me from behind curtains. That was quite alright with me, so Esmeralda and I pushed on. I could see in my rear view mirror this pick-up truck coming up behind me. The truck pulled up beside me with its hazard lights flashing. The two men in the truck asked me what I was doing, and I told them I was walking to California. They said, "You got a long way to go" and pulled off. I continued walking, thinking to myself, man, what was that all about? My mind automatically started thinking of what bad could happen. Secondly, I thought of how I could defend myself from an attack. As I pushed further, I could see up ahead a man get out of the truck and cross over to my side of the street. They were too far off for me to make out whether or not they were the same guys who I spoke to earlier.

"Being brave isn't the absence of fear. Being brave is having that fear but finding a way through it." Bear Grylls

"Man, it's a great day to be alive"

I could see as I got closer that it was one of the men from the truck. He had a bottle of water and some peanut butter crackers that he gave me. That was very kind of him to do that, thank God. I stood there and talked with him awhile. I asked him if there were any motels nearby. He told me that there's a bed and breakfast about seven miles down the road. I pushed on after thanking him for the food and water. But before I could get five paces he said, "Hold on." He walked towards me and handed me a ten dollar bill. I said, "WOW, my first experience in Pennsylvania and it's been great, God bless you, sir." I'm finding out that people are generally good and this is what I should expect each time as opposed to going to the negative side first. I made it to the bed and breakfast in this town called Rome. Walking through this town made me think of when I visited Rome, Italy as a young service member. The day was coming to a close with the sun going down and I was happy to reach my destination. I went up the stairs to ring the front doorbell and no one answered. I say to myself, "Noooooo!" Then I peeked into the windows and it was closed. Luckily there was a house next door, so I went over to see if they were the owners. I knocked on their door and it took them a long time to open it. I asked them if they owned the bed and breakfast next door, and they said no. Then they told me the owners lived down the road as she pointed to the right at their house. I thanked her and decided to walk down to their house without Esmeralda. With the sun going down I could walk faster without her, so I took Esmeralda around to the back of the bed and breakfast and headed off to the owner's house. All the while as I was walking there, I kept going over in my head what to say to these people. I really needed them to let me stay for the night. And then I remembered, *"Expect good and you will get good."* After making it to their house an older gentleman opened the door. I quickly explained to him what I was doing, my cause and that I was a veteran. I handed him one of my cards and told him that he could look me up on the computer and that I had been walking all day in the rain and I really needed to doctor my feet. By this time the wife had come to the door and said hello. As I explained myself to the wife, I really emphasized the kids and that I was raising money for them hoping it would help. The husband came back from googling me and they said yes. Bob and his wife Sandy gave me a ride back to the bed and breakfast and the husband told me that he was in the Army. We talked about basic training and where we were stationed. What I found out is that Bob was stationed in Baumholder, Germany six years before I was there. Serendipity, right? That was so cool that we connected using the esprit de-corps from the military. I felt very comfortable with Bob. Sandy showed me to my room and brought a baked loaf of bread and told me to help myself to anything in the house. They told me that they would be back in the morning to cook some breakfast. I said to myself, "WOW, they trust me, total strangers I just met a couple of hours ago." This was a five-bedroom newly constructed house. They also told me that their grandson the golfer might be coming in for the night, and he sleeps downstairs. I had a chance to meet their grandson that evening. He seemed like a pretty interesting young man.

"Once you choose hope, anything is possible" **Christopher Reeve**

"Man, it's a great day to be alive"

I was home alone. I got the chance to wash clothes and make a few phone calls to let family know where I was. My cell phone had no service, so Bob gave me the green light to use their house phone. I felt truly loved, like the Bible said *"if God so loved us, we also ought to love one another,"* 1 John 4:11. Bob and Sandy came back the next morning and she made breakfast while Bob and I talked about our times spent in Germany. The breakfast that Sandy had prepared was homemade pancakes, bacon and eggs; man, I got stuffed. I asked Bob what it would cost me to stay another day to give my body a rest day and catch up on some writing. He said it wouldn't cost me anything. I asked him, "Are you sure?" Bob said, "I don't need the money." Then Bob asked me when would I like to leave? I didn't want to take advantage of their kindness and told them the next day. So, I stayed two days with these kind people. I thought it was phenomenal that I get a chance to reminisce with someone that was in the same place overseas (Germany), at the same company, same barracks. Bob is the first person who I have met (35 years later) who was stationed exactly where I was stationed. It felt good to talk about it. As they were leaving, they told me that they would bring me a plate later on for dinner. I thanked them again. I spent the rest of the day going over my route with my sister Shawanna on the phone. She is my co-pilot for my route. By me staying the extra day in the very nice house I was able to relax my mind along with my body. I think a relaxed body is a powerful body, and a relaxed mind allows powerful thinking.

"Man, it's a great day to be alive"

I took off walking south on Route 187 to connect to Route 6 going west, and it was a nice day. I only walked around 17 miles and the clouds became gray as a few raindrops fell. I spotted a closed road on the opposite side of the street and headed for it. It was the property of a gas company which had an ideal place to camp. I just had to figure out how I could get Esmeralda's big girth around the gate poles because the gates were locked. I pulled her up and around the poles as I struggled to get up this small hill with her. Once I found a good spot and started setting up camp, the mosquitos swarmed down on me like the bees. I took out some Skin So Soft, rubbed it on and it worked for a little while, but they kept coming and wouldn't stop. I then put on my rain gear with the hoody and continued to put up the tent. After a few minutes I found the Deep Woods Off spray my sister gave me. I used that and sprayed a little in the air and they disappeared, thank God. While living in Albuquerque for the last 10 years I had no mosquitos because of the amount of rainfall. Man, I miss that.

"A good person can make another person good; it means that goodness will elicit goodness in the society; other persons will also be good." Bhumibol Adulyadej

"Man, it's a great day to be alive"

As I sat there eating with bug spray at arm's length I really enjoyed dinner. In the woods I'm constantly looking over my shoulder for a bear or any other type of animal. I finished eating, retired to the tent, then fell asleep. I was awakened around 11:30 p.m. to this loud cracking of thunder. It was raining like a Scud missile attack in the invasion of Iraq. The rain was really coming down, but I was dry in my tent praying it stopped by morning. Give glory to God, it stopped raining around 5:30 a.m. I got up and did my morning burial and ate some breakfast. I sat there in kind of a hypnotized state just listening to the morning sounds. I say hypnotizing because some mornings if I didn't get up and move after breakfast it would change my goal for the day. It always happens in the mornings, me not wanting to move. I thought of it like this; when you're working out, or just going to work sometimes you don't feel like it, but when you get there you say to yourself I'm glad I came or I'm glad I went. So, once I got started walking, I was so glad I did. The mornings are the most peaceful time of the day for me. I had just come to realize that today marks my 30 day anniversary for being on the road. Yes, only seven more months to go.

My walk that day started out going downhill, which was not so bad. But what goes down must come up. I found these truths to be fact. The weather was good, and I was clipping along pretty nicely with my long get down the road stride. Out of the blue I said to myself, is my cell phone bill due? So, I stopped and looked at the phone to see if I had any service. I didn't have internet service, but I had phone service. I continued trucking on. I could see a small gas station coming up and I was thinking about stopping to use the bathroom and to get some milk. I decided not to stop because it was on the opposite side of the road. I would have to go through a little more maneuvering to get over there, so I'm good. I did see a Black man come out and walk towards his car. We immediately locked eyes (and said to ourselves a brother, what the heck is he doing out here) and gave the universal upwards head nod to each other saying, "What's up." He went to pump his gas and I continued to push west. This situation made me think of an Iraqi soldier I'd trained. His skin was just as dark as mine or darker. When we first saw each other we did the universal head nod. I came up to a library following this route. I was in a town called Troy, Pennsylvania. I found it coincidental that I also walked through a town in New York called Troy (home of Uncle Sam). The building looked fairly new, so I pushed in to replenish my water and use the restroom. While parking Esmeralda I could see ladies who had just pulled in taking items out of their cars. I quickly pulled out my empty containers and rushed over to hold the door for the ladies entering the library. We spoke as each one passed me, but there was a few who stopped and couldn't take their eyes off Esmeralda. Now they were circling her taking pictures, and then one of them asked me, "What are you doing and what is this, she asked?"

"Curiosity is one of the most permanent and certain characteristics of a vigorous intellect" **Samuel Johnson**

"Man, it's a great day to be alive"

I told her that I'm walking across America for the Make-A-Wish foundation and this is Esmeralda. The lady again repeated herself asking me, "You're doing what?" Now more ladies were gathering and taking pictures of Esmeralda, and she loved it. I was starting to do the pee-pee dance when I asked one of the ladies where's the bathroom and she pointed it out. I returned and answered the basic questions most ask; where do you sleep, what do you eat, how many miles you walk a day? One of the ladies was the librarian who asked me for a card. I gave her a small piece of yellow notepad paper with my name, Go Fund Me web page, and Walkabout America all handwritten. She looked at the piece of paper I handed her and asked me if I would like her to type up and print me some new ones. I enthusiastically replied, "Yes!" She looked at me, smiled and said, "You know this comes with a price." I smiled back and asked what. She said that I would have to be their guest speaker today for their book of the month club meeting. She then asked me how many do I need? I said as many as you can give me. She said for me to go inside and meet the other ladies and get some of the food they made. They fed me with all those snacks and a few homemade things. Oh, I can't forget that there was 1 man there. I spoke to him before and after the meeting and he gave me one of his books he wrote. I really enjoyed myself talking to the book club. They made me the guest of honor for the day. I hung out for about 45 minutes with them and told them I had a date with the sunset as I headed toward the door. The librarian handed me about 75 cards she'd made up for me and I profusely thanked her. As I was headed west down the road, I came to this construction site that bottlenecked into one lane. The oncoming traffic had to stop when the light changed so that we could go through. Esmeralda and I had to walk behind a lady that just passed us who was at the book club. She recognized and waited for me as I parked, and made my way to her sitting in her car. She asked me if I had a place to stay and I answered no. She said that there are no hotels in Troy, and she told me that I could stay with her and her husband for the night. I agreed and got directions from her. She drove off and said she should be home by the time I got there.

A few miles later I finally made it to her place. She said I wouldn't miss her physical therapy sign out front on this main drag. I spotted the sign and crossed over to her driveway. She forgot to mention that her driveway went straight up, and it was loose gravel. Now Esmeralda weighed in around 200 pounds, so while pushing her up the driveway I would slip in the loose gravel and it was a work-out pushing her heavy girth up the hill.

"Don't give up before the miracle happens" **Fannie Flagg**

"Man, it's a great day to be alive"

I got about halfway up and I could see a silhouette of a large dog at the top of the driveway. She didn't tell me about this either. It was letting me know in a low slow bark that this is his property. As I got closer, I could see that it was large (Big) Japanese Akita that was doing a combination of growling and barking now. I thought about my days as a letter carrier, what would I do. I pulled out some beef jerky and some sun chips and got closer. I was trying to see the sex of the dog so that I could baby talk it. So, I stopped (I figured out it was a girl). I ruffled the sun chips bag like I was going to give her some as I was baby talking her. She stopped barking for about three seconds. I dropped the food thinking that she was going to take the bait and I could get around her. She didn't eat the beef jerky or the chips, that I dropped and she got back in front of me barking. Esmeralda and I kept walking slowly and with confidence and no fear as I baby talked her. The dog was still barking, and the bark was starting to change. These barks were louder now, and I was thinking to myself, where is she (the lady that invited me)? She has to hear this dog barking. When getting closer I could see an orange flag on a lawn mower as it moved around in the distance. I'm thinking that must be the lady's husband. He stopped to see what the dog was barking at and to talk with me. The husband and I met, and the dog listened to his command. He told me that his wife had called and said that I would be stopping by to stay the night. She should be in shortly. He asked me how I got past her, pointing at the dog. I told him that I used to be a mailman for 15 years and I showed no fear and tried to feed her and used a little baby talk. He told me she is trained not to eat from strangers and she hates baby talk. The wife finally pulled up as her husband and I were talking. She kept apologizing and I told her no worries, "There are worse things in life." She went inside to prepare dinner and her older sister came over to meet me. Her sister told me that she had seen me earlier that day as well. The sisters were hard apple cider makers (in their spare time) and when I told them today marks my 30th day on the road, they said we must celebrate. They went down to her cellar and brought up four bottles of some of her apple cider. We ate dinner talked and exchanged stories while drinking apple cider. After about four glasses and I was really getting my buzz on, but I was tired, I told them I needed to retire for the night. Besides, my right ear had been hurting all day, and I thought something may be in there. The young lady's sister said that she was a nurse and she could help. She gave me some peroxide and a round light blue baby booger sucker thing (small suction ball with point). I went to the bathroom and started flushing my ear and lo and behold, I sucked out a dead bug. They all cheered when I came out and told them the news. I finally went to bed in a room they put me in downstairs. Today was a good day, thank God.

"I cannot do all the good that the world needs. But the world needs all the good that I can do." **Jana Stanfield**

"Man, it's a great day to be alive"

I got up the next morning and they were cooking breakfast, I could smell it. She yelled downstairs where I was and said breakfast is ready. I went up and greeted the both of them (husband and wife). The Big Japanese Akita lying in the corner wanted me for breakfast, not the blueberry pancakes she had made. Her husband had to lock her in another room. While talking with them they were telling me of a mutual friend they had known since the 1970s that would put me up for another night at their place if I was interested. I agreed. The husband called their friends in the next town (Mansfield) I was traveling through and made arrangements. The wife then asked me if it would be cheating by giving Esmeralda and I a ride down Mt. Everest (her driveway). I said heavens no. So, I packed up and she drove us down. As we said our good-byes and she drove off, a guy on a bike (cyclist) saw me going around Esmeralda before the walk, making sure she was buckled and snapped down. He seemed curious about what I was doing and stopped. He asked me if I was walking across America. I said yes and could see that he was on a long trip also. I noticed the saddle bags on his bike; it tells me he was traveling. Matt was his name. We exchanged stories, took pictures, and gave each other email information on the causes we were supporting. He took off shortly after that; besides, the temperature seemed like it had dropped. I continued to walk along Route 6 until I got to an old state road with less traffic and the serenity was wonderful. It took me about three miles around Route 6 and avoided a few hills. I eventually made it to Mansfield to the family's house the last couple set up for me. They were a very kind spirited couple that has a dog that looked like Benji and also two cats. The cats were freaking me out, because I'm not a cat person. So, with one of them constantly snaking around my leg it was driving me nuts. I kept saying to myself this is a temporary event in my life, I was the outsider coming in. The couple showed me to the room and gave me some clean towels. They said this was their daughter's room when she stayed here. I had a great night's sleep. I thank God that these people were so very nice to me. I sat at the breakfast table and had a very interesting philosophical conversation with the husband Mr. D. The wife had a prior commitment that morning, and was gone. We talked about some of the issues we had encountered with our dysfunctional families, and how we dealt with them. What I gathered from our conversation is that every family has pretty much the same issues. It doesn't matter if you're rich or poor, Black or White. Mr. D and I had a commonality which was that he and I were both in Chicago when Dr. Martin L. King was assassinated. Mr. D and I both talked about how we viewed the destruction of the city. I said this because I was a young Black child struggling with the civil rights issues. Mr. D on the other hand was a young White adult not really understanding why the city was being burned down and businesses being looted. He said that he and his young friend were so naïve that they were going downtown Chicago and was going to try stopping the people from looting the businesses, but the National Guardsmen and the police officers stopped them. My memory of that day was to get home with my little sister from school.

"Just because you don't understand it doesn't mean it isn't so." **Lemony Snicket**

"Man, it's a great day to be alive"

I finished up breakfast and took a shower. I loaded up Esmeralda and we headed west. Mr. D and his dog Benji decided to walk with me for a few blocks, which I thought was so cool. After Mr. D and his dog exited off like an Indy pace car, Esmeralda and I were back in the race. I gave him a hug and thanked him for opening up his home to me. We then went our separate ways. I could see this female letter carrier across the street up ahead and now she was coming towards me. I couldn't resist telling her that I had worked as a postal worker for 22 years. She stopped and we talked postal for a brief moment. It was great. That morning started out cool until I hit a couple of hills and warmed right up. The night before, we looked up the legal way to walk the roads in this state, cording to the law. We found the state law on walking the roads of Pennsylvania and it stated I had to walk into the traffic and not have the traffic on my backside. So, this whole day I had been walking against the traffic. It felt kind of frightening, but I'm sure there are worse things in life. I didn't have to keep looking down at the mirror when I walk against the traffic. That took some getting used to. I walked until I came to a school bus office and went inside to use the bathroom. I walked in and there were a bunch of people sitting around talking and waiting for school to let out. I asked to use the rest room and the youngest driver there pointed it out. I told them I was walking across America and they said wow. I came out of the rest room and they started asking me the standard questions about the walk. The youngest driver said, "I used to live in Monterey, California." He gave me ten dollars to buy lunch in the next town. That was very nice of him. I said goodbye and continued on. I made it to a town called Wellsboro and got a room for two nights. I was not feeling the greatest; my stomach didn't feel good and I felt a little dizzy. I couldn't wait to get to my room. I purchased a Mountain Dew in the lobby before going to the room. I got to the room, sat down immediately and drank it. As I sat, I started to feel a little better. I downloaded something from Esmeralda and ordered a pizza (with the works). The pizza came, I then took a shower ate and relaxed. The NBA playoffs were on and I felt right at home. I slept well. I was awakened with the buzz of my phone from a text from Albuquerque. It was a friend, they wanted a status report. I told them where I was and they responded, "Wow. You are a little over your 500 mile mark." Those numbers made me feel really good. This was something I had never done before in my life. I was so excited about it, I sent out a lot of texts to friends and family telling where I was and me hitting my 30 day mark on the road at 500 miles. Esmeralda and I were officially in the 500 milers club.

"Nothing in life is to be feared. It is only to be understood." **Marie Curie**

"Man, it's a great day to be alive"

I missed my goal of hitting Galeton today. I found a rest area in Rexford, and put up camp. It was a nice clean area off of Route 6 with a porta john in the distance which worked out great. I slept well and got up the next morning and ate some breakfast. I loaded up Esmeralda and started walking. The weather was very nice that day somewhere around 80 degrees. As I was walking facing traffic, a sports utility vehicle (SUV) pulled over off the road. Now the SUV was coming head on with me very slowly. Esmeralda and I stopped in our tracks. The vehicle finally creeped up to about 10 feet from me and a lady got out and said, "We saw you yesterday in the last town, what are you doing?" I told her and she said that's very nice of you and handed me twenty dollars. I told her thank you and gave her a card with the Make-A-Wish website on it. They drove away. I said to myself, wow, it's some nice people out here. I pushed on a little further and a red truck slowed down and the man driving yelled out of the truck window, "Hey, have you eaten anything?" I yelled back, "No." He said, "Meet me at the restaurant up the road a few miles and I'll by you lunch." I said okay. Just before I got there another gentleman stopped and asked me how he could help? I told him I could use some water. He said, "I'll meet you at the restaurant up the road." I said okay.

I finally made it to the restaurant and the gentleman with the water was waiting outside when Esmeralda and I rolled up. The gentleman handed me the water and some Gatorade, and told me that he owned a photography business. He wanted to take a picture of Esmeralda and me. He asked if it was okay to give to my cause and I told him about the website and gave him a card. I told him how to navigate through the site to my Go Fund Me page to donate to the Make-A-Wish children. He said, "Ok, I will, but I want to give you something right now," and he gave me a twenty dollar bill. I thanked him and made it inside. The couple in the red truck where there and waved me over. As we were talking, I found out that this gentleman worked in some capacity with the Make-A-Wish foundation. There again is that word: serendipity. Wow, God is good!

"I'm surrounded by nothing but great people. I've been blessed with that, so really, I've got no choice but to be an all-around good person." Tim Duncan

"Man, it's a great day to be alive"

I ordered breakfast and with me being a veteran they didn't charge me. They didn't know that I was a veteran when they offered to buy me a meal. They gave to the cause later via-internet. I had a great time with Earl and Sandy. Being out here on the road from day to day it's real easy to lose track of what day is what and I didn't know it was Memorial Day when I got up that morning. Today was a good day.

After eating, I took off walking west as the crow flies. I found a cabin just before I reached the top of this mountain road in West Pike. There was a very interesting man named Ralph he was 82 years old and looked well. He was getting around good and he liked basketball. After checking into to one of his cabins I turned on the TV to watch the NBA playoff. It was Cleveland-vs-Atlanta; it was a very good game. Cleveland beat Atlanta by one point. I found watching that game odd. During each commercial the TV would change channels by itself to tennis. I found out later that Ralph controlled the TV from his office and you were at his mercy to watch whatever he wanted to watch. Count it all joy it, could be a lot worse. This piece of property was very peaceful with a stream running along the back sides of all the cabins. Ralph had a picture of mama bear and two cubs on the property that he said used to frequent this place. His place also had a small pond where you could do some fishing if you like. I slept okay because my body was tired, and something was biting me all night. I woke up itching. I think the bed in the cabin had bed bugs. I didn't complain, it was a warm room with a hot shower, and I got to watch one of the NBA playoff games. Today was a good day, thank God.

"Man, it's a great day to be alive"

I got up the next day and took off. Today I finally conquered the 9 mile hill Mt. Denton. I didn't think it was so bad; I had been comparing all the hills I encountered to those character building hills I walked in New Hampshire. Mt. Denton was a good walk. New Hampshire's hills were at the top of the list so far. Mt. Denton did not go straight up; it leveled off in sections which made it tolerable. I was stopped twice by some passers-by and asked if they could take a picture with Esmeralda. I keep pushing until I reached the summit. It was only a 2,424 feet elevation push. I knew by the time I made it to California I would push up higher grounds than that. The downhill descent wasn't that bad either. I finally reached the town of Coudersport where they had the only McDonalds around. I ordered me a big fat calorie loaded burger with fries and a strawberry shake. It reminded me of a song from the 1970s by the Ohio Players, and the lyrics went like this; "Heaven must be like this, it must be like this." I sat outside and ate while talking to a young group of teenagers questioning me about what I was doing. Esmeralda and I took off to walk about another 13 miles and came to a town called Port Alleghany. It had been raining on and off all day.

"Push yourself again and again. Don't give an inch until the final buzzer sounds." **Larry Bird**

"Man, it's a great day to be alive"

Sometimes I would ask myself what is the purpose of the rain gear, because I stay dry until I start overheating and now I'm sweating. I sweat so much somedays I can pour sweat from the sleeve of the Patagonia rain jacket. I see why I have lost 15 pounds so far. I made it to a fairly new gas station which I thought was very clean. There was this lady that pulled up beside me and said that she had seen me in the last town of Coudersport and was curious why I was walking. I told her my mission and she asked if I had a place to stay for the night. I told her no and she insisted I stay with her and her family for the night. She said she would call her son who had a truck and he would give Esmeralda and me a ride to their place. They lived three miles in another direction that I was walking. But I figured I'm going to get a hot meal and shower out of this deal and make some friends.

Her son arrived and helped me load Esmeralda and we drove off to their house. The lady's other younger son was in the driveway shooting hoops when we pulled up. He was 14 years old I know this because when I met him he told me his birthday was yesterday. I told him what I was doing, and he opened up to me as though we knew each other for years. They allowed me to set up camp in their backyard. They were telling me that a bear comes out of the woods occasionally and goes through their burn barrel at the corner of their garage. Now the garage was beside where I had my tent pitched. I said to them jokingly, "I hope he doesn't like dark meat." We laughed and they told me that he wouldn't bother me. That's like when I was a mailman people would tell me that their dog doesn't bite. Her son came out of the house with some art project (which was right up my alley) he was working on for school. I complimented him on his work and showed him a few portraits on my phone that I had drawn. He had this one picture of his NBA star LeBron James that he said he wanted to draw. I told him to get a pencil and I would help him before it gets dark. I drew a quick picture for him of LeBron James and he loved it. He wanted me to get a job at his school as their art teacher. He told me the one they have now sucks. I laughed and told him to practice, practice, and practice. Because practice makes permanent and if you do this you will be a much better artist than I am. He kept saying he can't wait to show his friends this picture.

"Anything is possible when you have the right people there to support you."
Misty Copeland

"Man, it's a great day to be alive"

I told him that was my birthday present to him. Her other son who picked me up had gone to get his 3-year old daughter had now returned. The 3-year old asked her father why my skin was so dark. I laughed and told her that's how God made me. I told her father it was a good thing I agreed to come over. She gets a chance to experience something different. I asked if I was the first Black she'd ever met. He said yes and smiled. I think God places people into our lives to always teach us something.

"Man, it's a great day to be alive"

Today was a good day. I woke up around 7 a.m. and could hear Isaac from my tent leaving for the school bus. I rolled over, did my thing in the bottle and fell back to sleep. I was awakened again by a screen door closing; the lady of the house was letting her little dog out. I sat up and started doctoring my feet and got dressed. I went inside with the family to use their bathroom, brush my teeth, and to do my morning constitutional. I could smell breakfast cooking as I was showering. The lady's brother was over and he thanked me for coming by and jokingly said, "I would not have had a hot breakfast otherwise." The breakfast was very good and filling, but I had to make tracks. I couldn't get a ride back into town because her son with the truck had to go to work. Esmeralda and I made the push three miles back into town to get back on Route 6. The lady felt bad for me walking back into town, but I told her three miles weren't long in comparison to 3,000 miles I need to walk to finish. I only walked 10 miles and made it to a town called Smethport. I did a total of 13 miles with the 3 I had to do just to get started. I had run into at least six challenging hills today to reach this town and they had taken a toll on me. The hills in New Hampshire were still more challenging, even though I did have to fuel up (peanut butter) before tackling two of the hills today. As I was walking through the small town, I saw this man out working in his yard and I stopped. I asked him if there was a VFW in town. He said yes and gave me directions to get there. I made it to the VFW and parked Esmeralda and went inside. There were five people in there and the bartender. I asked her if it was okay for me to pitch my tent out back. She said yes, but she had to call and check with the commander. He said yes and he would be down later to greet me. I asked for a glass of milk and they didn't have any. She offered me a Gatorade instead. The drink was well welcomed, it was good. Other people started coming in and this one particular lady seemed to be afraid to talk to me directly. She acted as though I was going to do some harm to her. She would be one of those people that if you saw her walking on the same sidewalk (toward each other) she would cross over before we reached one another. I could hear her asking the bartender a lot of questions about me. And on one occasion the bartender had to come down to where I was sitting and ask me the same question the one lady had just asked her.

"The fear of being different prevents most people from seeking new way for solving their problems." **Robert Kiyosaki**

"Man, it's a great day to be alive"

I would answer the question leaning back out of my seat looking down to the lady who asked it. She wouldn't look at me. It was all good, I had enough people around me now with their curious questions. I even attempted to start a conversation with her, but she just seemed so guarded like I was going to harm her. Then she mentioned to bartender if it would be okay if she called the local newspaper reporter who she works with, to come down to interview me. The bartender asked me if I would be interested. I said sure. The reporter showed up and his name was Fran, a very easy gentleman to talk to. Fran and I talked for about an hour or so. Everybody there knew him and some of them had him as their school teacher along with their children when he worked in education. After the interview he wanted to take pictures of Esmeralda and me. Fran told me the interview would be in the local paper tomorrow. I thought that was so cool. I'd never been interviewed by a newspaper before.

I went around back and started putting up my tent for the night so that I could take my shoes out, relax and do some journaling. While I was back there a gentleman by the name of Troy came around and asked me if wanted to stay the night at his hunting lodge camp. I asked him if he had showers there and he said yes. The only thing is it was around three to four miles in the opposite direction that I'd just walked. I told Troy I'm not walking backwards, I'll stay here. He said, "NO! You deserve better. You're a war hero my fellow veteran brother. I will take you and Esmeralda in my truck and bring you back here for breakfast tomorrow." I then agreed. We made it to his camp and it was deep off into the woods. With natural gas flowing underground Troy stopped at his grate and walked over to turn the underground gas on. His house camp was located on 65 acres and it was beautiful. There was another guy who came out to the campsite from the

VFW also. He brought some beer with him and we sat around this huge campfire and talked. We could hear the frog orchestra warming up and it was getting dark. I hadn't heard these sounds in years. I didn't hear these frog sounds living in Albuquerque, and it was beautiful. One side of the pond the frogs sounded like a plucking of a banjo string. The other side of the pond they sounded like a long drawn out cello bass string and other sounds I was trying to make sense of.

"Feeling beautiful has nothing to do with what you look like. I promise."
Emma Watson

"Man, it a great day to be alive"

The thought of something happening out there crossed my mind when I could see I had no cell phone signal. I couldn't even text. If something would happen no one would know where I was. This is the chance I took for the serenity and beauty of Mother Nature. I stayed sharp and alert knowing I would not go down without a fight.

The next morning Mr. Troy was a man of his word and things went as planned. We went back to the VFW where they cooked breakfast for me and loaded me up with Gatorade before I left. I took off from the VFW with supplies and the morning paper. Mr. Fran did an extraordinary job with the write up about me and my journey.

"The greatest service that one can render to God is by helping others." Dr. Dennis Kimbro

I stopped at the Post Office on the way out of town and mailed my sister a copy of the article. As I was walking through town people were waving, honking their horns and some stopping to give me cash in support for my cause. The whole town was excited, one of the VFW brothers said the other night. He told me that by you coming through walking, you have inspired some of us to do something. I said thank you and all I'm doing is walking. I continued pushing Esmeralda for another 17 miles and made it to Mt. Jewett, Pennsylvania. Just before I got there a car pulled up in front of me and a young lady (13-14) got out of the passenger side. I stopped and she came closer. She told me that she had just got released from the hospital and was headed home with her mom. This young lady wanted her mom to take a picture of us shaking hands. I said, "Sure, let's do this." Afterwards she gave me a hug and a cold bottle of water. Her mother said that they had just read about me in the paper. That newspaper covered about five little towns along my trek down Route 6. I thought to myself, "Wow, the world is full of good people." What they (the Newspaper, and the VFW) did was to inspire me to stay even more positive and to keep walking. I could see that there was another VFW lodge up ahead. I crossed over and made it inside. The bartender said that the commander owns a restaurant/bar and hotel about seven miles up the road in Lantz Corner. "He wants to put you up for the night and feed you." I got a Gatorade from her (she didn't have any milk), and I continued on.

"Man, it's a great day to be alive"

As I was walking, a lady on the other side of the street was running trying to stop me and finally, she did. She also had just read about me in the paper and wanted to shake my hand and to say thank you for doing what you're doing. The reception from the people along the journey in this part of the world has been great. This is something that I didn't expect when training for this walk. I would say that the funniest and the most appreciative thing that happened that day was when a gentleman gave me a donation. I like to blast certain songs when I'm entering a town; that motivated me to walk even faster. This particular day I had the Isley Brothers cranked (signing *"Who's That Lady"*). I thought I heard a car horn but I wasn't sure and I kept walking at a pretty good pace. As Ernie Isley was jamming on his guitar (summer breeze) I could see this man running towards me. He had gotten out of his car and was trying to catch me. So, I stopped. When he reached me, you could tell he was out of breath, with his cigarette still lodged between his fingers. He said, "Man, you walk fast!" As he deeply inhaled and exhaled trying to catch his breath, I offered him some of my water and he said no thanks, as he started telling me a story about his granddaughter. He told me that she was a Make-A-Wish recipient and was granted a wish. I said, "Wow that's amazing." This made me feel very good inside knowing what I'm doing will help another child like this gentleman's granddaughter. He said to me that there should be more people like you and handed me three dollars.

That was the highlight of my day. I still smile each time I think about it. It's the people that are really impacting my soul.

I eventually made it to the motel, met the owner and got the room and a bite to eat. I showered and relaxed for the evening. Today was a good day.

"Man, it's a great day to be alive"

I got up and decided not to walk today. The rest to the body in a clean relaxing environment felt really good. It also gives my mind a break from being alert to the dangers of walking with traffic. Mind, Body and Soul, this walk was a complete package. After walking over to the restaurant to get something to eat I came back to the room. I e-mailed some friends and family about the newspaper article that I was still excited about. I lay in the bed watching the weather channel and fell asleep. Today was a good day, thank God.

"Man, it's a great day to be alive"

I woke up early and felt rested. I walked for about six hours today and the entire day I couldn't stop thinking about how there are still good people in the world. I strongly believe that what you think about will happen. I reached my goal today and that was making it to Kane, Pennsylvania. There I met a guy by the name of Bob who pulled up beside to ask if I had lunch. I replied no. He said that he would get me a sandwich from Subway a little further down the road. "What would you like on it?" I answered and he instructed me to wait for him at the thrift store up the street and the owner's name is Ed.

I made it to the thrift store and met Ed. I didn't think any Blacks lived here. Well, I was wrong: Ed was as black as me. He told me that he was born here into a mixed marriage and had been here all his life. Bob finally came in with the sandwiches and as we ate them, we somehow got to talking about the Army. He told me that he joined the Army in 1977 and did basic training at Ft. Leonard Wood, Missouri or as he said, "Fort lost in the woods," MO as it's universally known. There's that word again: serendipitous. I told him that I did basic training there in 1977 also. And that we could have been passing one another in the early morning during physical training (PT). I thought to myself, Wow, we had a great conversation. I then told him that Esmeralda and I had to keep on trucking before the sun fell on us. Today was a good day thank God.

"Man, it's a great day to be alive"

I didn't make my goal yesterday because it started raining on me really hard and the lightning strikes were very scary. The visibility was also very short for cars to even see me, until they were right up on me. That was getting too close for comfort; I'd already had a few close calls today. I was somewhere on a road between James City, and Russell City, getting pelted with these huge raindrops. I thought to myself I have to get off this road. I found a spot not far off into the woods and pitched my tent. I figured the rain will stop by morning. This was my first time putting up my tent in this heavy downpour type rain. I'm here to tell you that it's no fun. Your equipment is getting wet, you are wet, and the food you decide to eat will be wet also. And on top of it all you get inside the tent with all this wet gear on. Then once inside out of the rain your yoga classes begin. From the Crane/Crow (Bakasana) to the Half Spinal Twist (Ardha Matsyendrasana) yoga pose is what it seems like when taking your clothes off. Trying to do this in a one-man tent was very uncomfortable. Once I was out of the wet clothes and into a dry sleeping bag I was comfortable. I think that we have to get uncomfortable to be comfortable. Today was a good day, thank God.

"Man, it's a great day to be alive"

I woke up to the same rain that stopped me in my tracks yesterday. It was raining cats and dogs and I had to do my morning constitutional. I got out of my dry underwear, put on my hat, shoes, and rain top then headed outside. With my baby wipes tucked under my arm I did what I had to do. I figured no one would see me because I was back off in the woods and it was raining like the jungles in Vietnam. I did my duties and went back to the tent.

Man, I would have never in a million years thought that I would be doing what I'm doing today. I'm finding out that these humbling experiences are giving me more clarity and direction. The experiences also are a key component of me completing my goals to be successful every day. Living one day at a time

While in the tent I got dressed, ate breakfast, and then took down camp. With the rains slowing up it gave me a chance to drag Esmeralda's soggy bottom out to the road. Pushing Esmeralda in the rain is a little more challenging because she takes on water like the Titanic. I headed west and stopped at a USDA Ranger station to use the rest room and talk to the employees. After all, I was retired from the Forest Service and whenever the moment presented itself I used it. It was still wet outside and the rain was intermittent and a little cool. I found the entrance and went inside and introduced myself and told what I was doing. They had me sign the guest registry. I enjoyed speaking to them. I took a picture with Smokey the Bear they had in the lobby and continued on. It had been raining on and off all day with these scary lightning strikes. I couldn't stop I wanted to hit my goal today. I hit my goal and got a motel room. I was wet and cold from the walk when I finally made it to the room. Once I got everything in the room I needed for the night I ordered pizza and walked over to the gas station and got some milk. Today was a good day, thank God.

"Man, it's a great day to be alive"

I took off from leaving for the day later than I'd planned. The owner of the motel was a talker, but a good man so I listened. I ended up leaving an hour and a half later from Marienville, Pennsylvania. I walked 8 ½ hours that day attempting to hit my goal of making it to Tionesta, which had a couple of motels.

"Man, it's a great day to be alive"

I continued walking that day unit it was 8:30 p.m. I had my flashers on walking down a curvy hill in the dark. It made no sense, but I had to hit my goal. I made it to a park along this fast running river. I set up my tent in this covered sandbox, and a porta potty was not far away. I started setting up camp in the dark. I was a little disappointed for not hitting my goal. My goal was to be in a nice dry and warm motel room. But that's okay, I'll just reset my goal.

The next morning I decided not to walk. I'll take the day off to dry off and dry out some equipment. The sun came out and it was much welcomed. A man on a motorcycle pulled up and I began to talk with him. I asked him how far I was from town, and he said right across this river. I started laughing. It's all good, I had a chance to dry out, relax and save some money. I talked the gentleman riding the motorcycle into going to town and buying me a Subway sandwich. He was a little reluctant to do it at first and then I told him that I would give him $5.00. He went and got it for me. I pulled out my Ohio map and started looking at it. Each state I walked through I ripped out the entire page of the giant atlas. Then I would highlight the route I would walk around 20 miles out. I then folded the map to fit inside a gallon Ziplock bag for easy access from my cargo pocket.

This way gave me a much more organized and precise thinking on which way to travel. I would read it like a book and study it day and night. I also used electronics when they functioned. Because with solar if there's no sunlight I'm dead in the water and there were many days with no sunshine. I always knew which way to go, even when I didn't know which way to go. I will be in Ohio soon. So, as I sat there writing with my head down engrossed in the journal not focused on anything around me I heard a noise. I looked up and there was a dog standing about 15 feet away. It was an older Rottweiler, and it looked a little confused. His under belly was wet and I immediately thought it swam across the nearby river. I could see the back of homes on the other side of the river thinking he came from over there. Anyway, Esmeralda and I wanted to be alone. I stood up and gently shooed him away with my hand gestures. I continued writing and recharging my batteries. It was a better day then yesterday weather wise. The sun was out more today which gave me a chance to juice up my solar panel. Today was a good day, thank God.

"Man, it's a great day to be alive"

The next day I packed up Esmeralda and headed for Oil City, Pennsylvania. We only pushed 6 ½ hours that day because of the hilly terrain. I was stopped by a lady waiting in her driveway who told me that she had seen me in another town yesterday and wanted to give me a couple of cold drinks. I thanked her and gave her a card. I had been getting a lot of bottles of water from people today. I counted them at the end of the day and had 27 bottles. That was one short of a case believe it or not. Now Esmeralda was already jam packed with what she brought, and with more water added that made her that much heavier. I didn't turn down any water, though, because I didn't know from where I would get my next drink. I pulled out the insect net hood head protector and walked with it for a few miles today. Man, I looked like a big black bee keeper pushing Esmeralda! I can remember passing by this one house with this little girl riding her bicycle in the driveway. She stopped and stared at me like I was the first Black to walk on the moon. I smiled and gave a downward head bob and kept on trucking. The hood worked well, I wasn't taking any more chances with something getting in my ear. I made it to Oil City and got a room. At first the manager said he had no rooms available. I kept emphasizing my cause with the Make-A-Wish foundation and how far I'm going to complete this goal. I finally persuaded him, and he put me up in one of his rooms he had turned into a storage room. It had a couple of air conditioners in there, but I didn't mind. It had a bed and shower. After I got settled in and showered, I walked across the hotel parking lot to a McDonalds to get me a milkshake.

"We live in an age that stresses personal goals, careers, happiness, work and religion." Mother Angelica

"Man, it's a great day to be alive"

As I was standing around waiting on my order number to be called the man who was in front of me asked me out of the blue, "Do you work out?" I discreetly sucked my stomach in and my chest out and said, "Yes. I have been for the last few months." Now this guy looked to be around 70 something. He then asked me if I would be willing to play on the senior's softball team there in town. I told him no, I'm just passing through headed to California by way of walking. He said, "Wow!" and started with the usual questions. I answered them and gave him a card with my website. I could tell this guy was a talker; he started telling me about the history of the town. I told him that I had just ordered a pizza (which I did) and it was on its way and I left. I went back to the room where I had some clothes soaking. I was taking advantage of their laundry at the hotel by washing clothes. I received the pizza and went back upstairs to get my clothes out of the dryer. After returning to the room I started to relax a little bit, eat pizza, and was looking at the weather channel for my travels tomorrow. Then I get a knock at the door and it was Mr. F, the 74 year old I'd met in McDonalds. He wanted to know if I wanted to take a tour of the city, and I told him no, I was tired and just wanted to rest. We talked for a while and he told me interesting facts about Andrew Carnegie working in this town, and how he went back to school at the age of 56 to get his four-year degree. Andrew Carnegie with his philanthropy work for helping others is inspiring alone, but Mr. F's accomplishment of going back to school when he did, my hats off to him. That is a huge fear factor that thousands of people face each day. That is; thinking whether or not their age will be a factor or if you can still learn new tricks as an old dog. These factors keep people from living their dreams. I had to push him out of my room to get my clothes that were in the dryer. Mr. F and

I exchanged phone numbers and he went on his way. That was a very interesting man who is not letting age define what he should be doing. Today was a good day, thank God.

"The most courageous act is still to think for yourself. Aloud". Coco Chanel

"Man, it's a great day to be alive"

Today I only walked around 15 miles due to the hills. I found a place on the side of the road which I thought was a very tranquil spot. It looked to me like an entrance into this type of wildlife conservatory and had these huge elephant ear type of plants cropping up all over the place. That with the overhead shading from the trees gave this spot such a tranquil feeling. The local deer like to eat these plants. Once I set up camp, I heard a sound in the distance and it was a deer. I didn't want it to get any closer to me so I stood up to scare it away by raising up my arms to make myself look bigger, but the deer kind of just looked at me for a quick millisecond and continued grazing. As I stood there like Dr. Jack Griffin the invisible man, I shouted at one deer, "I have faced a bear and I'm not afraid of you." So, I grabbed my baton and quickly extended it and started whacking a tree beside me a few times. The deer still just looked at me (didn't faze him). I sat back down and said to myself if you come any closer; I'm going to kill you. The white tail deer finally got his fill and spring hopped away.

As I sat there looking around I was in awe of God's beauty, just at peace with the world. Then I heard a car pull up and a man got out and started suiting up putting on fly fishing gear. About 75 yards east from where I was camping was this small running creek, which was where he was going. As he walked by me, he didn't even look around, so he didn't even see me until his trip back. I held up my hand as he was walking to his car and said hello. I asked him if he had caught anything and he told me he'd only caught one fish and had to move higher upstream. I finished eating and hung my food up in a tree away from my tent in case there were any bears in the area. I had a great night's sleep.

The next morning I could hear another guy pull up and could see he was going fishing also. He saw me, and we exchanged hellos as he continued on his way. I made a cover overhead as I hid behind Esmeralda and a few bushes to do my morning constitutional and then I ate breakfast. I then eventually got all packed up to walk. While sitting there digesting my food, I got to thinking how peaceful this place is. I said to myself, "I could stay here a few days and just write." Just as that thought evaporated from my brain I just happened to look up and there was this snake hanging from one of the tree branches. I said to myself, "Wooo, I guess it's time to get to stepping," but not before I could get a closer shot of it with my camera. While I was zooming in with my camera to get the shot, I could see this large lump midway down the snake's stomach. I'm thinking that this snake is in no hurry to move. It probably took out one of these squirrels frolicking from tree to tree. Today was a good day, thank God.

"Man, it's a great day to be alive"

Today is one of my sister's birthdays. I prayed that she has a great day as I walked around 17 miles today and again, I had to trek some hills that slowed me up. I made it to Sandy Lake, Pennsylvania and stopped at the gas station to use the restroom and get a bite to eat. A gentleman in there said, "I saw you in the last town. Why are you walking?" I'd been getting that a lot on this walk; *"I saw you in the last town."* I told him the what, when, where, and why I was doing what I was doing. When I went back outside to comfort Esmeralda there was this young lady looking her over. She saw the Make-A-Wish embroidering and started telling me about her niece who was granted a wish and then she handed me $30 for the cause. I told her thank you and handed her a card. I had to walk another two miles off the main road to get to the park where I would be camping. There was this swarm of tiny flies that congregated in clumps of at least a thousand that kind of hung in the air right where I was walking. I stopped to retrieve the bee-keeper hood looking thing to put on my head, and kept on trucking. After reaching my two mile mark I stopped at the first campsite off the side of the road to set up. While setting up along the river a vehicle pulled up in the area and stopped. A young lady jumped out of the back of the truck running over towards me and screaming in a giggly way. They had seen a snake about to cross the road, and she was trying to catch it before it got away. I shouted out you guys see a snake, they said yes. I told them not to let it get away, I'll get my camera. The snake was about three feet long and black. I could tell that it wasn't poisonous from its movement and the head of it. I used my baton to hold him up while the girls took a picture of me and Mr. Snake. Cool, the snake excitement was over. I walked the snake across the street and let it go into the weeds. I went back to setting up camp. I started a fire and it helped smoke away the flies and mosquitos, and then the clouds rolled in and the rains came pouring down. I had just finished eating and I went inside the tent to stay dry. I did some reading and writing and eventually I fell asleep. I was awakened around 3 a.m. by this long-neck crane doing some frog hunting. I then realized I had food in my tent from falling asleep earlier and not hanging it up before the rains. I moved the bear spray and 45 Annie closer and went back to sleep. Today was a good day, thank God.

"Either you run the day, or the day runs you." **Jim Rohn**

"Man, it's a great day to be alive"

Today was the birthday of my other sister. Yes, their birthdays are back to back, that's pretty cool. I prayed that she had a great, safe, blessed healthy productive day as I walked these 20 miles. I walked by a driveway today which had a small American flag hanging on the post upside down. I stopped and took out my duct tape and stood the flag up correctly on the post, quick fix. Now by the time I got to the other end of the driveway the owner had walked out and we met. He asked me what I was doing around his mailbox. I told him that the American flag was hanging upside down and that I had friends over in Iraq that had died for this flag. I'm a veteran who had made sacrifices for the military also and the flag hanging upside down was disrespectful, so I was correcting it. He was wearing a hat with an eagle and a flag on it and I asked him if he was a veteran. He said no and started telling me about someone in his family who was in the service. He then started apologizing and giving me an explanation for why the flag was hanging upside down. Really, the driveway you pull into every day, and you don't see this flag? Come on. That's what I was thinking to myself. He began thanking me over and over again for my service. His wife had come out by now with two ice packs to keep my drinks cold, and offered them to me. I told her no, I have no room for them, (besides, it makes Esmeralda heavier), and I continued moving forward. Man, it feels good to know that you can stand bold when doing the right thing.

With me moving forward it took me up this strenuous hill which zapped all the energy out of me once I reached the top. I made the command decision to sit there and eat lunch. It was much needed. I made it to Greenville, around 5:45 p.m. and the Clark motel where I was going to get a room, but it was closed. There was a note posted in the door window saying they were at a family emergency. I stopped a man walking and asked him of any other motels in the area. He told me that was one about five miles in another direction. I did not want to do that, so I decided to continue walking until I got out of town and put up camp. As I was walking along the sidewalk, I passed a restaurant owner who was out hosing down his area on the sidewalk. He stopped and asked, "Where are you going?" I told him, and he told me to stop, come in and have a couple of hot dogs on the house. I thanked the gentleman and told him that it would have to be in a to-go bag. I'm attempting to beat the sunset. I got the hot dogs and pushed up this really hard huge hill just as you leave town. Getting to the top was a much focused slow hard push, and it was exhausting. Today is a great day, thank God.

"The good life is to be earned with hard work and sacrifice." **Dr. P.T. Chia**

"Man, it's a great day to be alive"

After leveling off and getting my breath back I walked past this man working on a truck in a large mechanical shop. I could see that he had a very big back yard, great for camping. I stopped and told him about the hotel being closed in town and asked him if I could camp out in his back yard and he said yes. Jim and I talked for a while and I went out back and set up camp. His area was a great choice because he had no direct neighbors and a small wooden shop further back. It looked like he had about 3 to 4 acres that he was sitting on. I liked the small wooded part that meant I could get up in the morning and do my thing without anyone seeing me. Jim finally came around and asked if I needed anything, and told me he would leave a side door unlocked for me to use the restroom. Man, that's great. I've only known this guy for a few hours and he has trusted me with his workshop. He said he was leaving for the day and would be back in the morning. Jim lived across the state line. I asked him how far the state line was from here, and he said around six miles, YES! I slept very well, and when I got up I felt very well rested. I spoke to Jim who had come back. He told me a story about how his property was sitting on an old salvage yard and when he digs around the property, he sometimes finds old car and truck parts from the 1930s. We said our good-byes, and I headed for the state line. I had to encounter a few rolling hills and one more Pennsylvania hill that was about a ¼ mile up just before entering Ohio.

I made it to the state line around 11:45 and it was a nice and sunny day. I took my usual selfie with the state welcoming sign and was exploding with excitement inside, like those pop rock candies we used to eat. My goal was to make it to Warren, Ohio, which was around 27miles away which had the nearest motel. As I walked, I noticed the road was starting to flatten off, and I could feel myself becoming a flatlander, which felt great. No more strenuous New England hills.

"It is important that when we make a resolution, or establish a goal, that we take the Action necessary to accomplish that goal." Steve Maraboli

<u>What Pennsylvania means to me;</u>
Pennsylvania, Pennsylvania having the first zoo
Even Benjamin Franklin moving forward
Knew what to do.
Pennsylvania being the 5th state,
The Amish friend that I met
Fixed me a plate.
With Hershey's Chocolate's smelling fine
I will remember this place
As I walk across the finish line.

Chapter 6

Ohio

"Man, it's a great day to be alive"

I keep thinking to myself that I can cover more ground each day now. I finally made it to Warren, and got a room around 6:30 p.m. The motel was rundown and not very clean, like me and Esmeralda, we fit right in. I said to myself, *"Tony, there's worse things in life."* I enjoyed the experience and met some very interesting people there. I had a warm place to sleep and I had a warm, dry place to eat pizza, and this all gave me a warm fuzzy feeling. I called my cousin Nolen Roddy in Cleveland, to let him know I'd made it to his state of Ohio. I asked him if I ordered some supplies for the walk, would it be okay for me to send them to your address. He said yes. I asked him if he would find me on my walk and bring them to me. That was my proposal and he said, "I'm only 40 minutes from you. Why don't I come pick you and Esmeralda up and bring you to my place, to get some home cooking and hang out until the package arrives? Then I can bring you back to Warren for your restart point to continue walking."

I agreed with him. I applied the, "mastermind principle" which Cousin Nolen is a part of. He was very instrumental in helping me carry out my plan. My "mastermind alliance" will be compensated for all that they are doing for me. I have dropped a couple of the members from the alliance that were not on board with the plan of imagination. It's kind of like finding that mold poop on a rotting orange, or a bad tomato, or a potato. You have to get rid of it because it will destroy the other ones in the bag. People are the same way if they got that stinking mold poop fuzzing around them, get rid of them, or they will rotten those around them. I will be picked up tomorrow for some Rest and Relaxation (R&R) while waiting for a package, which will be a blessing. Today was a good day, thank God.

"Make it a habit to tell people thank you; and to express your appreciation, sincerely and without expectation of anything in return." Ralph Marston

"Man, it's a great day to be alive"

I got up the next day and ate what left-overs I had and I shaved and showered. I danced with Esmeralda to get her out of the door and I finished packing her up. I could hear the housekeeper making her way down to my room to clean. I had Esmeralda all packed outside the room, so I gave the housekeeper my key and waited for Nolen and Pearl out front of the room to arrive. They came around 11:30 a.m. Nolen and I loaded up Esmeralda and strapped her down like a wild bull wanting to break out of the gate, in the back of the truck. There was a McDonalds on the way out of Warren, so we stopped and had lunch. As we got into Cleveland there were some places I saw that really looked rundown and bad.

The neighborhood where Nolen and Pearl lived was very nice and neat. They lived in a cul-de-sac circle plot with a very fine house and yard, which was very nicely maintained. Nolen and Pearl seemed to be doing well. After we got settled in, Nolen and I went out to get something to eat. We got some chicken wings and ribs with a little cole slaw. They eat like my mom and dad, which is they don't do vegetables like me. I was the only one who ate the cole slaw.

Count it all joy, I'm very thankful for this opportunity, "there are worse things in life." They went out to run some errands for the day. They let me use their washer and dryer and while waiting for my laundry I sat behind their pearly white baby grand piano and plucked away at the keys. When they returned, they had their grandson Chase with them. He was not expecting to see this gray bearded man in the house, but after the 3rd day together he and I were the best of friends. I showed him how to spell his name by signing, and I drew a picture of one of the Ninja turtles for him. I showed him pictures of my granddaughter Aalyiaa. Nolen has this

177

vast knowledge of our family's history on my father's side. My grandfather and his dad were brothers, and his mother and my step-grandfather, on my mother's side were cousins. He even had pictures and some valuable heirlooms that have belonged to his family for several generations. He showed me this one Booker T. Washington coin which I thought was so cool. Had I stuck to my plan of walking and him finding me on the roadside with the supplies, I wouldn't have had the time to learn family history from my great cousin. I hung out with them at their place for five days. All the items that I expected arrived Thursday and I agreed to leave that Saturday. It was a very relaxing, refreshing, recharging, reunion with Cousin Nolen and Pearl. Pearl's children came by one evening and we had dinner together. That was a great experience and fun. Today was a good day, thank God.

"Take a deep breath… Inhale peace, and Exhale happiness." **A.D. Posey**

"Man, it's a great day to be alive"

I was really ready to start walking again. I felt like a thoroughbred horse waiting to bust out of the starting gate to dash around a muddy track. The day they took me back to the restart point it was raining. That morning my cousin and I were up early, kind of looking out the window and listening to the rainfall, and he looked at me, and I looked at him and said I have to get this party started. The rain will stop one day, I have to get to California by December.

The rains finally stopped. We unloaded Esmeralda; Pearl wanted to feel how Esmeralda handled on the road. She asked me if she could push her for a few steps. We were at a park and the road wasn't as dangerous for her. I let her push for about 25 yards or so walking alongside her giving her instructions on what to look for when traffic approaches, and how to drive Esmeralda. We encountered a small hill and I could see she was getting a little winded, but she insisted on marching on, which was a good thing. I have learned from John Wayne that "quitters never win, and winners never quit." She said afterwards it took a lot of focus on so many different things going on around you. We exchanged love and said a prayer, and Esmeralda and I boogied on down the road. The mini vacation in Cleveland with family that I'd met for the first time was wonderful. I extended an invite for them to visit me in Albuquerque. Today was a good day, thank God.

"Energy, drives, enthusiasm & dedication is encouragement & inspiration to others." Stephen Curry

"Man, it's a great day to be alive"

I'm headed towards Deerfield, Ohio today. That day I walked for about six hours and I stopped to refuel because after the rain stopped, the weather got really hot (80 something degrees) and muggy. I saw a spot off the side of the road which looked like an abandoned farm barn/shed. As I pushed down on the handlebar of Esmeralda to pick up her front end to turn her, the front wheel popped off. I said to myself, "Wow, God has my back." This was a great spot for this to happen. Esmeralda was a little embarrassed as I picked up the wheel and pulled her crippled butt along this dirt/weedy road to the abandoned barn. After making it to a nice spot around back of one of the buildings where no one from the road could see me, I set up my chair and sat in it. I was little hot and dehydrated. I sat there for a long time and drank plenty of fluids before making a move to repair the front wheel and setting up camp. The day was still early; it was around 4:30 p.m. I finally got my strength back and fixed Esmeralda's front wheel.

I decided to explore the area, so I took my weapon out and walked to the other barn. The area was overgrown with weeds and I was hoping not to step on a snake of some kind, or even more frightening the area had a prison break and I didn't want to be surprised by an escaped inmate. I could see the shed was used because out of the three tractors two of them had flats, and the one that didn't looked workable, and the land around the barns had been worked. I even saw a rafter of turkeys (earlier while sitting quietly hydrating my body) far out in the worked fields. I decided to camp out in the barn and deal with the owners if they showed up. As I got everything set up in the barn and was about to eat, I saw a movement out the corner of my eye off in the distance. It was a ground hog/woodchuck that popped its head out of the dirt and looked around. I very loudly cleared my throat to get its attention. He made a groundhog sound and

180

went under like Caddy Shack. He popped up in another corner of the barn with his wife to show her to me. I again made a noise and threw something in their direction and they went under again. I covered the one hole closest to me with some weeds I pulled from the outside. They stayed down for a while after that; after all, I was the outsider on their turf.

There was this smell in that place like a mixture of oil and animals that seems to be imbedded into the dirt floor. It's hard to describe, and it was starting to give me a headache. So, I went into my tent when the rains came rolling in again. The high winds along with the thunder and lightning were very loud, and with a combination of the tin roof on the barn flapping and banging all night made a loud night sleeping. I still happened to sleep well during the night and was awakened by the noise of the groundhogs squeaking, playing from hole to hole. Today was a good day, thank God.

"If you don't have confidence, you'll always find a way Not to win." Carl Lewis

"Man, it's a great day to be alive"

As I was getting ready to start my day, I went outside the shed to do my morning constitutional and suck in some fresh morning air. The air outside that barn smelt so good in comparison to that stale air inside. I went back inside to finish zipping up Esmeralda. I had to put some cologne on my bandana to help with the smell. I don't know if it was worth the sacrifice of being dry. I had a headache for almost the whole day. It quickly subsided when the rains came in after reaching Alliance, Ohio. The rains were coming down so hard I couldn't see to walk. Esmeralda was paralyzed, so we just stood there and I took it like a man, a wet soggy man.

After the rains slowed down enough to see I started walking. A car goes by and hits me with a wave of water big enough to surf on. With my wet paints married to my skin from the rain I made it to State Street and went east of my route on 183w about three miles or so. I took the sidewalk and got soaked all over again from other passing vehicles. I accepted that and kept moving. The last three blocks of the sidewalk ran out. As I stood there thinking how best to maneuver this oncoming traffic, I knew it would take too much energy to cross the street. I could see the sidewalk continuing on the other side of the road. And then once I got down far enough I would have to cross back over to get to the motel. I started walking into the traffic, and I'm doing my best to alert the cars that are coming towards me. I would grab Esmeralda's skinny white flag-pole and rock the orange flag vigorously back and forth to get the driver's attention, and did I mention no shoulder on the road. As I'm walking, I say to myself wow, this is risky business, and it's like playing Russian roulette with this oncoming traffic. I'll never walk this road again. I finally made it to the motel. I downloaded some items from Esmeralda, covered her and tied her to a pole outside the room like she was a horse.

I ordered a pizza and chilled for the rest of the evening. Today was a good day, thank God.

"The sunrise never finds us where the sunset left us." Unknown

"Man, it's a great day to be alive"

The next morning after drying out from the rains, I took off walking back up the same street I got soaked on the day before. I made a decision to walk down the middle of the 4-lane road. The sun was out and there was no rain. Walking down the middle turn lane worked out a lot better. I had to switch lanes to the far right when I came to a light, but overall it was a much smoother journey walking back the three miles to route 183w. I thought of what Muhammed Ali once said when I was walking that risky no sidewalk, no shoulder the day before. He said. "He, who is not courageous enough to take risks, will accomplish nothing in life."

Sometimes your courage must overcome your fears, and it worked. The walk to Minerva, was a comfortable 6 ½ hour trek. I spotted a good place to camp. There was this church that had a small wooded area beside it that I could tuck myself away in and still be noticed, that's where I camped for the night. I set up camp and ate some pizza slices from the night before and washed it down with a bottle of Cool Blue Gatorade, the name describes itself actually. Tastes just like blue. I took my shoes off and read some of Napoleon Hill positive action plan and could see in the distance rain coming in. I got up and placed the tarp over Esmeralda after putting all my gear in the tent, and the rains rolled in. I think it rained all night. The thunder and lightning woke me up around 4:30/5 a.m. and it was still coming down out there. Around 6:30 a.m. it stopped. My plan was to walk nine hours today to get to Dover. I found it to be unique to walk through two towns that have the same name but in a different state. I walked through Dover, New Hampshire at the beginning of the journey, and now Ohio. I had reservations at a Comfort Inn so that I could see the NBA finals. I ended up walking 10 ½ hours. This was my longest walk since I'd begin and my body was tired. I got a room and the game was starting in about 30 minutes. I then ordered some food and took a shower. I should have taken a hot bath to relax my muscles and help them recover, because I didn't sleep very well last night. I paid for another night here to help my muscles recover and write in the journal. I even had a chance to look up Mr. Willie T. Clay who walked from Cincinnati, to San Diego, California in 1960. I found his contact information on social media and left him a voice mail. Mr. Clay is the author of "The Big Walk," one of my inspirational role models. Today was a good day, thank God.

"When you endure things with patience, you attain all things that God can give you." Teresa of Avila

"Man, it's a great day to be alive"

I woke up and thought how Esmeralda would be with a different front wheel on her. I took off the spare underneath Esmeralda and replaced the bad wheel. I decided to do some general maintenance on her since this was a down day. I rearranged some items in the cart to see if I could pack it better, and in doing so I had to make a hole in the material with one of my sharpest knifes. I was thinking as I'm making a hole in the material with the point of the knife gouging into it, if I'm not focused on the right thing, I could cut myself. And as fast as that thought come to mind, I pushed my sharpest knife throw the material and cut a good gash on the top side of my left pointing finger, or index. I immediately stuck it into my mouth so that I wouldn't get any blood on the carpet. I un-snapped the first aid kit and went to the bathroom to run some water over it and stayed calm. After cleaning it I could see that it should have been stitched up. I stopped the bleeding and tightly wrapped some gauze with a small strip of duct tape around it. I also think that a cut like this to my non-dominant hand was a way to help me stay focused. If there was a next time it could be worse. I just can't drive myself to the emergency room if I hurt myself out here. Dr. Arthur Parrot my cousin tells me each time we speak my journey word for the trek is FOCUS, and he spells it out one letter at a time to me. I continued replacing the wheel and repacking Esmeralda. My phone rang and it was my dad. We had a good conversation and I told him that I loved him and I appreciated him being my father. The next day I walked about 7 ½ hours and along the way I could see this influx of Amish cyclers on the road puddling past me with a bewildered look. They would only speak if I initiated it with a head nod and a smile or the wave of the hand. As I walked further I could see some type of huge factory that employed those cyclers because I saw some of them coming out, it must have been a shift change. It rained on and off all day. This part of Route 39 shoulders were not so favorable, they sucked. The bad road edging ate away the rubber on the wheels, especially the front one. I came to an RV campsite during the end of my route for today. I pulled in with excitement of outdoors in a rather clean environment, but I was told no.

As I pulled up a lady was leaving for the day and she told me she had no washroom facilities for me to use. She said she only have full hook-up for RV's. She pointed me out to a park down the road through town maybe a mile out. I made it to the park, but to get into the park I had to walk down this short but very steep hill/driveway with Esmeralda. That's no fun; all she wants to do is run down the hill. I had to restrain her temptation to roll down freely on her own by gripping her handlebar and slow walking her down. The park worked out well, it gave me an area to protect myself from the rains. I set up camp under this picnic area gathering with tables and electricity on the poles.

"I got a theory that if you give 100% of the time, somehow things will work out in the end." Larry Bird

"Man, it's a great day to be alive"

As I was relaxing in my chair with my shoes off, I decided not to set up a tent for the night, but instead blow up my air mattress with sleeping bag and sleep on top of one of the tables. While finishing up dinner my phone starting making this unusual buzzing and then a voice saying, "This is a national weather alert, take cover; there is a tornado warning in your area." I said to myself where am I going to take cover. I curiously looked up at the sky and watched for an oncoming tornado. All I saw was the rains from a distance rolling in. The rains came and I stayed dry underneath the picnic area. What a welcoming to Berlin, Ohio. Today was a good day, thank God.

The morning started off dark and gray with rain dropping on and off. I walked down Route 39 until it came to township Rd. 557 south. My map was showing me if I went down this road, I could save myself two miles and then connect back with Route 39 which would eventually take me back to Rt. 83. This would be the scenic route with an occasional Amish horse trot and driver going passed. It was a very peaceful road. I was supposed to make a turn onto another unmarked road that should have connected me back to Route 83 but I must have walked right past it. I did stop at a fork in the road where I realized I had to recalculate. I didn't want to get too lost on those unmarked back roads so I continued on 557 and came to a village called Charm. It was a few Amish shops, and a cheese factory alongside a Swedish restaurant that stood out to me. I came upon this Amish gentleman on the side of the road selling wood-crafted items he had made, and we talked. We had a decent conversation about life and things.

The rains had been chasing me all day and it finally started coming down. I could see down in the distance some welding going on in the back of the hardware-like store. I asked the older Amish gentleman if he thinks they would help me and Esmeralda with her back wheels. He said sure they would and highly recommended the hardware store. Just as I made it down to the hardware store, I could see the two guys in the back garage welding. I threw up my hand and said hello. They responded the same looking at me as though I was an alien with three heads walking towards them. I made it around back and explained what I needed for Esmeralda to strengthen her rear wheels. Elijah the welder and I agreed on a plan of action to strengthen the rear wheels in order for me to complete the rest of the journey. It took him around two hours to finish the minor surgery on Esmeralda's rear end. I looked around the shop and saw the hard rubber iron spoked wheel that would be great for the front of Esmeralda.

"When you come out of the storm, you won't be the same person who walked in. That's what this storm's all about." Haruki Murakami

"Man, it's a great day to be alive"

It was a heavier wheel, and Mr. Elijah put his word on it, that it would make it to California with no problem, and will not wear down. I had this surge of pleasure come over me knowing with the work done on this machine that it will roll all the way to California. I was dumbfounded when I tried to take a picture of the crew who was fixing Esmeralda but Elijah told me they don't pose for pictures. By me attempting to make small talk I really felt like the outsider. I jokingly ask one of the young men his age. He told me 16 and I responded with, "You must be in the 10th grade." Then again I was educated by Elijah that they only go to the 8th grade and after that they learn a trade of some type and live there traditional life. Strike two on me with my ignorance of the facts. Okay, I understand, so I thought. The last thing I did to embarrass myself was to attempt to give them a tip (money) after they finished when Esmeralda they wouldn't take it. Good thing they didn't take it, because they stuck me up for $180.00. Wow, I thought they would help a brother out. I'm still happy I made the decision to give Esmeralda a makeover because it's going to benefit the both of us. Man, it's a totally different world where there are different people, it's a great contribution. I camped out in Clark, Ohio on Township Rd. 19. Today was a good day, thank God.

"You're always one choice away from changing your life." **Mac Anderson**

"Man, it's a great day to be alive"

Yesterday after the work I got done on Esmeralda it set me back time wise from hitting my goal. That's okay because I can always reset my goal. I got up from the campsite off the main drag and it was raining just like yesterday, which ended up raining all day long. Despite all the rain, there was some satisfaction out of the ordeal which was the sound of the horse trot. I thought that sound was a very beautiful relaxed rhythm. That repeated pattern of movement accompanied with that trot that I would hear from a distance, was great. My mind always thought of a metronome doing its beats per minutes on top of a piano. I saw this one horse and carriage pass me in a nice relaxed trot going downhill. I could see how the horse was making an adjustment with the carriage slightly pushing him down the hill, and never getting off rhythm. I thought to myself, "Wow." God knew what he was doing to create that animal to do that. I really thought it was amazing to witness that. The Amish folks in the carriages would always look at me with that very curious suspicious eye. I would think that because of me walking with (Esmerelda) this cart with all my belongings and the fact that I am a Black man with a white beard, this looks a little different to them. They would always wait until I gestured hello, and they would follow suit by extending a welcome of some type. Count it all joy. I came to this one farm and I could see a farmer with a container in his hand walking and we happened to catch eyes. I gestured hello and he did the same as his two little kids came running up to him and looking at me with that shy curious eyes too. He held up his container and said, "Water." I pointed at myself as though I was in a crowded room and Esmeralda stopped. I think she said to herself, "DUH" we are the only ones on this road, dude, so go talk to him. Esmeralda and I turned towards his fence line along the road and met the Amish gentleman. He took one of my water bottles and went down to a spring that spit out water from the side of the ground into a brook at the end of this side of his property. The water was very cold and good. He introduced me to his children ranging from 5 to 11 years of age. He asked what I was doing, and I told him I was walking to California. He then turned his attention on Esmeralda. Yes, she was the ball hog again. He wanted to know the type of framing, the wheels, who did the stitching, how much does Esmeralda weigh, and do I have a phone? And do I have a phone! That question threw me for a loop. An Amish gentleman asking me, (someone without a car), do I have a phone. I reared back like I was dodging a fastball pitch with eyebrows raised, and said, "Yes. Do you have a phone?" He said yes, he has one in the barn, and would like for me to call him after the walk. I thought wow; this is what it is all about, the universal love and kindness that God blankets all. Today was a good day, thank God.

"Man, it's a great day to be alive"

The trek to Coshocton, Ohio along Route 83 today seemed long. I had a few challenging up and over blind hills and a few blind corners. I can tell some of the drivers were really surprised to see me when they come flying up and over the hill. I noticed that most drivers who drive up and around a curved road like to speed up, either going into the curve or leaving the curve, or both. This to me so far seems to be the second most dangerous things on this walk. I say that because I could be in that curve when the vehicle decides to accelerate right at the curve, and I could be squashed like a bug. Each time I faced a situation like that I would pray that the driver focused on the curve and not on me walking. The number one most dangerous thing on this journey is the lightning strikes. The majority of the time I didn't know what to do. As the rains fell and the thunder pops, sometime sounding like an Iraqi bomb I continued walking. I was telling myself if I keep moving, the lightning wouldn't hit me. Ya right!

A young man by the name of Alex stopped and asked me where I was going and if I needed a ride. I told him I was going to California, he said, "Where?" I told him that I was walking across America. He said wow. I asked him if he wouldn't mind taking a picture of me in this soaking rain to show my sisters. After he took the pictures he asked if I wanted some food. He had just come from a high school graduation party. He gave me a plate of food and I stood there in the pouring rain soaked eating that food. It was much appreciated for the energy I needed to push up the small hills I was encountering. As I kept walking, I would always be thinking about the road over flooding with all the rain that was falling. I walked past some spots that were right on the border of running over. The water everywhere was running fast. Five miles or so down a little further a small white car honked at me to stop. I stopped and it was the young man who gave me a plate of food earlier, and he had his girlfriend with him and a bottle of Gatorade for me to drink. The couple was very kind and offered to pray with me. As we were standing there holding hands a truck came by and we got drenched with water. I told them welcome to my world out here. They left me with a cross of some kind, and we said our goodbyes. The day was getting late and my feet were tired, and I was dripping wet. I came to this motel that was reasonably clean and convenient for me to get to Esmeralda when locked up outside. I ordered my usual staple, pizza from a gas station down the road. Today was a good day, thank God.

"Waking up sober is a good day. I love being able to wake up and do positive things, to go to the gym." Rodney King

"Man, it's a great day to be alive"

Today is Father's Day. I wonder what my boys think about me today as their father and what I'm doing. I'm not walking today, I think I will do a two day dry out, but for now I'm going over to Bob Evans and have some breakfast. Bob Evans was a short distance from the motel, and it was packed. They had people standing outside waiting. I checked in for a party of one under Tony and sat down. I spoke to a couple that was sitting there waiting and they were called for their table. A few minutes later the waitress came back out and said that the family she just seated wanted to know if I would join them, and I said yes. I made it to their table, and they asked me if I was on vacation. I told them what I was doing, and they wanted to hear more about the journey. They insisted on paying for the meal and I graciously received it. The older gentleman at the table gave me 20 dollars and told me to buy some supplies. The Spirit of God is all over the place. Today was a good day, thank God.

It's the day after Father's Day and my goal today is to make it to Dresden, Ohio, home of one of the world's biggest baskets at 48ft. long / 23ft. high /, and 11ft. wide. It was a good day for walking. As I was making trek down route 16 a white SUV pulled off the road and was waiting for me. I always had some reservation walking up to a total stranger's vehicle. I finally reached the SUV and the lady driving was someone (hotel breakfast worker) I'd met at the hotel a week ago in Dover, Ohio. She got out of the SUV carrying a drink in her hand. It was a milk shake from McDonalds. I was shocked to see her. I thought she was cute when I'd first seen her at the hotel as we flirted with each other. She was the kind of person who likes to give hugs. A person not being around touch for a while, those small common things as a hug makes me have a happiness that's hard to describe. She was on her way home coming from a doctor's appointment with her mom and dad. She said she drove past me earlier going to the doctor and thought about getting me something on the way back. That was a very kind thing to do. She introduced her parents and we hugged. The strawberry milk shake was right on time and the milk helped my muscles recover. There are very kind people in this world, and in the world, people are kind. The agape love of God blankets this part of the world today, and I love it. Today was a good day, thank God.

"Man, it's a great day to be alive"

I continued walking Route 16 and came up to this company entrance with this massive block of stone with words carved into it. I thought it was a cool piece of art. What made the stone carving so remarkable was the company's impeccable safety record that was etched into it. I pulled Esmeralda closer to the stone with me so I could examine the piece closer and take some pictures, but she resisted. She didn't want to go into the grass, and for good reason. She was like a big woman with heels, on sinking in the soft grass with each step. As I finished up, I pulled Esmeralda out of the grass and tried to turn her to line her up with the road to start walking. When I did that I noticed the rubber around the wheel came a ¼ of the way off. I said out loud "O no," but don't panic, think. I grabbed the crowbar I had attached to the side of Esmeralda and carefully got the rubber back onto the rim. I got off the main Route 666, yes 666, the locals here say three-6's. I met a local man at a gas and shop store and we made conversation. He told me he was a preacher and had a gift for me in his truck. I went to his truck and he gave me about eight small wooden crosses that I hung on Esmeralda. He wanted me to pass them out to others along my journey. Just before I left, he and his son who was in the truck prayed with me and they drove off. I couldn't help but notice that the preacher was packing a .380 on his hip. I thought about wearing my sidearm as I walked, and then I thought about how much trouble it could possibly bring, and decided not to. The state park that I was trying to get too had flooded from the rains we'd been getting. As I started down the road heading out of town I met this young lady and her three little girls standing out beside their car waiting for me to walk past. Each one of the girls had a one dollar bill in their hand. It looks like the mother is teaching these little girls compassion/empathy for another human being (wow, that is so cool). I introduced myself and the young lady asked what I was doing? As I was explaining to her what I was doing, but not quite all the way finished, she kind of interrupted the last sentence, and before I could put a period on it, she asked, "You a veteran?" She had read the Army swag I had sown on the front of Esmeralda, and I said yes. She went into telling me how she was married to a veteran and Iraq changed him for the worse. She went on to tell me more horror stories of when she was married to this veteran. I told the young lady that Iraq changed me also. I no longer have the marriage I was in for 21 years because of that stinking war. I went on to tell her that this walk helps me with my PTSD, and is a big reason why I'm out here doing this Walkabout-America. We held hands, prayed, (after all, we were on Rt. 666) and went our separate ways. I had to find a place to sleep for the night since the state park was flooded. Walking along the route I saw a spot going up off the road with a lot of overgrown vegetation. I pulled out my baton and scouted the area. I had to open up this gate that appeared to have not been opened for years.

"Be humble, believe in yourself and have the Love of the world in your heart."
Michael Jackson

"Man, it's a great day to be alive"

I was on someone's property; now I'm trespassing. I made it to the peak of this road, and this was the best spot. The view was great overlooking the river and part of the small town. I went back down and grabbed Esmeralda by her front end and pulled her up this very overgrown road/path. I could only do three steps walking backwards at a time because of the tall weeds and Esmeralda's weight. The pull up the hilly path took a lot of energy from me (which I didn't have) after a long day's walk. The sight on top of that hill was very peaceful, beautiful, and worth it. I set up my chair and ate dinner before I set up my tent this time. I felt I needed some energy and a little rest to even set up my tent, because I was really exhausted after the pull up to this campsite. I would use the same chair to watch the jets stream across the sky before the sun sets that day. Today was a good day, I thank God.

As I got to the campsite, it felt good. It was a nice warm summer day here in Zanesville, Ohio. I had a very good trek today. There was this road construction which had traffic thick and some bottleneck spots. I could see that the area of road where the workers were the busiest. It was in the far right 4th lane which they were repairing. I said to myself, "I could walk on this new black smooth road and not worry about traffic." All the traffic was creeping by in one lane and they couldn't drive on the newly laid road yet. The road looked like it was hard enough to walk on. So, I asked the lady that was standing there doing something (talking to another female) if I could walk down this newly paved road and she said she would have to find her supervisor. I told her to tell her supervisor to find me, and I took off on this freshly paved road with no distractions. This road construction went on for miles. I walked seven miles or so on it and never heard from her supervisor. My GPS was taking me off the main drag (this nice smooth new road) about two miles into another direction to a campground. Once I arrived to the campground I had to call the owner, who was somewhere on the grounds. He met me at his office and told me he didn't have shower facilities, and I told him that's quite alright. The gentleman who goes by the name "Bubba" only charged me $5 for the night's stay. As he was leading me down to my area, I spotted a couple with two children and I spoke to them. They returned the kindness back to me. It's something about the campground family of folks; we seem to all get along for the most part. I told them what I was doing, and they told me that they knew someone who had a wish come true. They offered me some pizza that they just had ordered, and I said no thanks, I have something. I didn't want to take food from the children. I set up camp and ate a sandwich I had bought earlier from Wendy's four hours ago. As I sat there after my meal, I spoke to a gentleman that was working the ground helping out (Bubba) and we had some good conversation about life. He and his girlfriend gave me some canned goods before I left the campgrounds. Today was a good day, thank God.

"When you're good at something, you tell everyone. When you're great at something, they'll tell you." Walter Payton

"Man, it's a great day to be alive"

The owner passed by my area and asked if I needed anything? He was going home for the evening. He stays in town. I told him I could use some bread for a sandwich. He returned with two slices of bread in a Ziplock and a small bag of ice, which was right on time.

The next morning while I'm sitting in front of my tent eating breakfast, a man comes out of one of the campers nearby with a dog on a leash. As he walks his dog past me I shouted out, "Nice dog." He kept walking as though he didn't hear me, and I know he did. He had a white pit bull terrier (the pointed nose Target looking dog) puppy. He took it back inside his camper after it did what it had to do and came out with another dog that appeared to be about the same age as the other one. I didn't learn my lesson earlier and shouted out again, "That's a nice dog too." It was a black and brown German Shepherd. And again, he kept right on trucking as though he didn't hear me, and I know he did. This time I said to myself, "fine, I don't want his stinking negative doodoo energy over here anyway. It's his loss." He seemed a little cautious about talking to me. Then later once he heard about what I was doing he put his guard down and came over to talk. He told me he was from Louisiana and people come up to his car all the time wanting something, and I thought you were trying to get something from me. I said, "No, sir; I was just being kind and speaking well to you about your dogs."

He said, "I apologize, man, I was wrong" (he said it, I thought it). "Can I make it up to you by giving you a fishing pole?" I said, "No thank you, man, I don't really fish."

He kept on insisting, "I'll give you my best one!" I then agreed and we walked over to his truck. He must have had at least 50 poles in the back of his truck all intertwined like a bounce of snakes tangled up. He carefully separated one and it was a fly rod. I looked at him and said, "Man, I don't know the first thing about fly-rod fishing." He said, "It's not hard, follow me." I'm saying to myself while walking down to this stream nearby, what have I got myself into? He gave me my first fly rod fishing lesson 101. I took the gift he gave me, and zip tied it to the side of Esmeralda. I told him when I find that perfect fishing hole along the journey and catch the first fish on this Walkabout, I would send him a picture. I think the young man learned something today just as I did. The couple that offered me pizza earlier came to my little spot and asked if it was okay for them to contact the news media about me. I said I don't mind, yes. They did, but the news media person couldn't make it today and wanted me to stay another two days here at the campground. I told them thanks for the kind jester, but I had to get down the road, west. Today was a good day, thank God.

"I'm not telling you it's going to be easy—I'm telling you it's going to be worth it." Art Williams

"Man, it's a great day to be alive"

I walked for about six hours and 48 minutes or so and arrived in a town called Somerset. Today was a 20 miler. It was starting to get late and I was a little hungry. I was trekking along looking for a decent place to put up camp for the night, when I saw this 3x5 foot Army Strong flag draped over the outside of this property's fence. There was this almost perfect spot just on the other side of the fence on the property. So, I began walking up this long gravel driveway to the house to get permission to set up camp in his yard for the night. I came upon a man cutting grass on a riding mower in the far corner of his back yard. I stood there like a deer on the side the road wondering whether I should walk out closer or wait until he sees me, after that row of grass he was cutting. I met him halfway and explained to him what I doing and over emphasized that I was prior service with the Army and he said sure, no problem. He went on to tell me that he wasn't a veteran and that his son is over in Kuwait. I told him that I've been there twice. He told me once he finishes up his lawn; he would come down to see if I needed anything. Thank God it worked out.

Route 22 was a good road to walk on, I think. It had more good spots along the way than bad ones. The owner came down to where I was and gave me a little history about him and his property. This gentleman was younger than me and he had gone through a divorce. He told me what helped him get through the aftershock and depression was working with wood. He ended up building this house with a little help. I thought that was amazing. He told me something that stuck with me to this day; he said, *"You have to get uncomfortable, to be comfortable."*

I asked him, "What do you mean?"

He said, "I went through a very uncomfortable divorce and some aspects of the building of this house. Now I'm reaping the benefits of being very comfortable in my life." He went on to say, "You are doing the same thing."

I looked at him and said, "How so?"

"Well, you told me you went through a divorce after returning from Iraq, and that must have been very uncomfortable, along with some parts of this trek that you're on. You told me walking helped you with your PTSD, but you just didn't walk around the block, you're doing it on a grand scale by walking across America. In the end you're going to have a much more comfortable life than you ever imagine."

"The more you seek the uncomfortable, the more you will be comfortable."
-McGregor

"Man, it's a great day to be alive"

I thanked him for the kind compliment and him telling me some history of this area. He told me that the area here where you chose to set up camp used to be a through and under. He went on to explain that this is where the cows would cross underneath the road coming out from the farm and graze. The gentleman told me that sometimes he thinks that he should have just purchased two acres of the land, because it takes up too much of his time caring for five acres by himself. Now I could have not approached this gentleman if I didn't have Positive Mental Attitude (PMA). I think that PMA is the fundamental desire of faith that gives you that extra something to step out into something unseen. I have read in one of Napoleon Hill's books that *"Great men and women have never found the easy road to triumph. It is always the same old route-by way of hard work and plenty of applied faith."* The next morning it was raining when I got up. I could hear the wrestling of the gravel through my tent, as the truck got closer to the end of the driveway, where I was camping. The gentleman was leaving for work. During my seven hour walk today I had to take a detour, because of construction on a bridge that was closed. The detour added three miles to my original 18.5 mile goal for the day. I met a lady who stopped me and gave me some fresh berries she had just picked down the road. She was curious about what I was doing and started questioning me. I explained and she thought it was great. But I could hear it in her voice with her questions that she was very afraid for me because of the dangerous roads I was walking on. I told her no worries; I have God on my side. My mind always goes back to the bridge in Oil City, Pennsylvania which I still think was very dangerous and one that I would never walk again. I continued on for a few hours more and a man stopped me on the road and asked if I was Tony? I said yes and he told me that he wrote for the local newspapers and would like to interview me tomorrow. The gentleman took a few pictures and drove away. I finally reached the motel that I had called this morning, but it had a NO VACANCY sign lit up hanging on the inside of the door like some Christmas ornament. I said in a loud voice "Oooo NO!" I was really tired after walking all day. I rang the doorbell serval times and no one came. So, I give her a call on my cell phone and she answers. Right from the tone of her voice I could tell she had taken a negative pill. She answered the phone and said, "Yaaa, what do you want?" I told her my name and asked her does she still have a room that she said that she had earlier when we spoke? She said, "No, I'm full." I asked her if I could camp out in her grass and she said no. I asked her of any other motels in the area, she said, "I don't know," and hung up on me. I looked at the phone in my hand as though it did something wrong. Well, I had to go to Plan B, which was to start walking.

"Stay focused, go after your dreams and keep moving towards your goals." ~ LL Cool J

"Man, it's a great day to be alive"

I looked up another motel on my phone and it was a two-hour walk around six miles. This I didn't count on, so the best thing to do is walk. As I'm walking this nice big heavy duty Ford truck creeps up slowly beside me. The driver of the truck yells out, "Are you a Vietnam Vet?" I said, "No! I'm an Iraqi Vet. Does that count?" He asked if I needed a ride. Man, God is good all the time. I said YES! And he pulled over. He helped me load Esmeralda onto the back of his truck, but not without a struggle; she was heavy. I told him the name of the other motel and he knew exactly where it was. The fellow Veteran took me to the other motel across town which worked out great. We unloaded Esmeralda off the back of the truck like we were holding a lady's hand while assisting her down some stairs. I noticed right away that I had lost one of my waterproof gloves that I had strapped onto Esmeralda. The winds from the drive must have blown it loose as we were driving over. The gentleman offered to drive back the way we came to see if he could find the missing glove. He called me later and said he found the glove in the middle of the street. I was so thankful to him. He brought it by before I went to sleep. He also gave me a six pack of beer which was very kind of him. That beer lasted until I reached Oklahoma. Today was a good day, thank God.

I got up early and called the newspaper man that wanted to interview me. He and his wife came by my room and took me to Bob Evans for breakfast. On the way to the restaurant I saw a Walmart and asked if we could stop, I needed some items. They were very kind people and stopped at Wal-Mart for me. The interview went quite well. We had some great conversations about life and the journey I'm on. After the interview they gave me a ride back to the route I was on and dropped me off. He told me that he would mail my sister a copy of the paper for me to read once I reach Illinois. I started walking to Circleville, Ohio where I had called the night before and made reservations. Besides, it was my motivation to make it to a paid room. On my way I had a close call with the traffic. I was walking across a small bridge with traffic where the shoulder disappeared, when this car coming up from behind me saw me and started to slow down because it couldn't get over right away to pass me. There was this semi-truck coming in the other lane that would be crossing the bridge at the same time as me. Now this impatient driver in the vehicle behind the one that was slowing up for me decided to come around both of us. The impatient driver realized that they were in danger with the oncoming semi-truck. The driver floored the gas pedal of the car to make it across just before the truck made it. This car was so close it came within inches from me. I could see the passenger's eyes as she put her hand and forearm in front of her face anticipating them hitting me. I was saying to myself, this is the day I'm going to get hit as I kind of braced for impact. Just as the car blew past me I did that bullfighter's wave with my hand and shouted TORRO! It didn't happen; I'm still alive thank God. That was the day I changed underwear. LOL

"You may never be fearful about what you are doing when it is right."
Rosa Parks

"Man, it's a great day to be alive"

Before heading out for my 7 ½ hours walk today I contacted the VFW in the next town and asked them if I could campout in their back yard. I got no answer, so I left them a message and told them what I was doing. I hit my 7 ½ goal and it felt great. Sometimes, I had to unleash the power of self-discipline and do things in a repetitive motion to get it done. I think the repetitive motion pushes us to succeed and to do things that failures don't want to do. And do them over and over again, hitting goal after goal. I say this in conjunction with me saying walk one hour at a time over and over again. By doing this I hit my walking goals every time. During my 7 ½ hour walk today I met a lady who stopped me at the gas station and handed me a McDonalds bag, and she made it clear that there is a gift card inside the bag that's worth $50.00. I thanked her and gave her a card. This was another kind gesture that God has sprinkled down on this journey. I finally made it to Fairfield, Ohio and I turned on my GPS for the VFW from my phone. It felt good to get there. As I was walking towards the VFW the commander of the post (169) pulled up alongside of me, and said they were all waiting on me to arrive. I entered the post thinking if I can get on the bartender's good side, I got it made. The welcoming was very comfortable, genuine, and at ease. I walked around and introduced myself to each and every one there. They asked if I wanted a beer, and I said sure. The bartender asked what I would like, I replied, "A Heineken please."

She said, "We don't serve that," and then I said, "I'll have a Rolling's, it's in a green bottle." I smiled and thanked her; I was on her good side. They had food there kind of like pot luck meals and it was good. The commander (Phil) and I sat and talked about our military service in our glory days. He told me that he researched me to see if I was the real McCoy and I panned out to be. He told me of a story of a veteran who came through, depleted

209

their funds and was a fake. The commander said, "You are legitimate, you have 900 miles under your feet. You're too legit to quit."

I said, "Hammer time." We laughed and he handed me an envelope with 35 dollars in it from the Amvets. And then he handed me another one from his chapter with 150 dollars in it. I told him that he didn't have to do this, and he said that I was a brother in arms and we have this camaraderie, and, "besides, you were at war, man, that speaks volumes. I wish I could do more." I thanked him and walked out back to set up my tent for the night. Today was a good day, thank God.

"An early morning walk is a blessing for the whole day." ~ Henry David Thoreau

"Man, it's a great day to be alive"

I woke up around 6:30 a.m. and lay there thinking what this day would bring. I also thought about what the commander asked me last night; would I walk in the parade with them today. Around 8 a.m. the commander of the post came in. I got up and went inside to use the washroom and to clean up. I decided not to walk today but to participate in the 4th of July parade with the post. I went back to the tent, gutted Esmeralda to pull out my red walking shoes, and took off for Fairfield, Ohio's annual 4th of July parade with my brothers in arms. This would be my first time participating in a parade as a civilian. I'd been in many military parades where I had to do the "Eyes Right" thing and then salute. The members were really happy I decided to march with them. We arrived and lined up behind the vintage Corvettes. As I was standing there in a little formation talking with other Vets, I felt very proud of the men I was surrounded by and what they had experienced. The secretary grabbed my arm and he took me where the local news person was talking to someone in this parade. I had seen the reporter earlier walking around interviewing other people. He told me after we introduced ourselves that he would do a small piece on me. He then asked me to meet him in back of his TV van in 15 minutes. I met with him and we spoke, but I felt like he didn't really want to interview me about what I was doing. After the short interview I thanked him and took off to catch up with the squad of soldiers I should be walking with. As I walked past all the different floats and people marching in the parade I would wave my hand at them and wish them a Happy 4th of July. I would occasionally hand my card out to someone in the parade. This one guy I handed a card to shouted out to the crowd that was gathered alongside the street watching, "Hey, this man is walking across America. Let's hear it for Tony!" This gentleman was 80 years old and was in impeccable shape. He stood about 6 foot 4 inches, very toned and was on this three-wheel type skateboard which to maneuver he had to sway his body in a side to side motion. That in its-self would be a workout for a young man to do. I think if I would have planned this parade walk with my fellow soldiers better, I could have brought Esmeralda along, she is going to be upset. If Esmeralda was here with me people standing along the street and sidewalks would get a better understanding of my mission and how I was accomplishing it. I finally caught up with the VFW Post and those guys looked a little tired, it was a very warm day. One of them said, I was wondering how we were going to find you, you're a fast walker. We went back to the post and someone started to barbecue. The commander was headed out to get something from the store and I asked if I could tag along, he said yes, hop in. I needed some items for Esmeralda's repair. Today was a stand-down day for rest and repair. After returning from the store we ate, and I went outside to do some maintenance on Esmeralda. That evening people that left from the post earlier came back to watch the fireworks from the VFW parking lot. It was a great last day to spend walking in Ohio with newfound friends. I will be in Indiana tomorrow. Today was a good day, thank God.

"Success is getting what you want, happiness is wanting what you get." ~WP Kinsella

<u>What Ohio Means to me</u>
OHIO Ohio, it rained all day
The sun didn't come out for anyone to play
My socks are wet, my shoes are soaked
Which one of these hurts the most
I walked in the water, I walked in the rain
I leave this state in a little bit of pain
With the lightning strikes afar, and the rumbling of thunder
Sometimes you didn't know what you were under
Ohio has been good
Ohio has been great
This is another state I can wipe off my plate

Chapter 7

Indiana

"Man, it's a great day to be alive"

I walked for about 20 miles today. I finally reached the state line and crossed over into INDIANA, the boyhood home state of President Lincoln. I had entered Mt. Carmel, Indiana. As I crossed the state line I didn't see the traditional green and white welcoming sign. My phone was telling me we were in Indiana. There was this house with around four guys standing and sitting out front when Esmeralda and I passed. I waved at them and they waved back. One of them asked what are you doing and I told them. They flagged me over and offered me two cans of beer and wanted me to tell them a story. I asked if there was a green and white welcoming to Indiana sign around. They said yes, it's down the road about a mile. We spoke for a while and I continued on my journey looking for a good spot to camp. I made it to the welcoming sign and did my pertinent selfie pictures by the sign. There were no motels in town, so I found this cornfield that was almost perfect. I pulled Esmeralda down behind the corn and set up camp. After eating, I sat resting in my little chair and day-dreaming about how this spot I'm in right now would look with a house over and along the stream. This farmer looked to have over 100 acres and I was thinking if I could own no more than 25 acres here it would be heaven on earth. Then I snapped out of my little day-dream and said to myself, this is not the first place I've dreamt about on this 78 day journey so far. I got up to walked down to the stream when this farmer driving a tractor I think saw me, after all I was on someone's property and it might have been his. When I suddenly saw the farmer after popping up from behind the corn where Esmeralda and the tent were comfortably hidden, I froze in my steps like a deer being hit with car headlights, thinking he wouldn't see me if I didn't move. I had just blown my cover. The distance from the road and me wasn't that close so the farmer might not have seen me, but I'm not 100 percent sure. After I went down for the night while lying in my tent, I heard the farmer firing his shotgun in the air. I then heard another farmer shooting in the air in a different direction, and then a third in a different direction. Now all kind of things are running through my mind, like the farmer must have seen me and called the locals and told them. I was thinking that by them shooting in the air was their way of telling me to get off the property. I can't see this happening every Sunday night. The shootings went on for about 30 minutes or so and stopped. Then I was awakened later by their shooting again around 11:30 p.m. They dispersed a lot of rounds within the short time. Today was a good day, thank God.

"I enjoy life when things are happening. I don't care if it's good or bad things. That means you're alive." Joan Rivers

"Man, it's a great day to be alive"

I pulled out of the cornfield around 8:30 a.m. and started my walk early. I wanted to get off this man's property as soon as I could. 8:30 a.m. will be the earliest I have ever started a day's walk since starting this journey. The walk to my next destination was a good one. I had no pain anywhere and the weather was good. It rained a little and stopped, but overall it was good conditions for a walk. After walking for around seven hours I got to the edge of a town and unplugged my phone from the solar panel to look up lodging. There were two bed and breakfasts that popped up. I called the first one and she wasn't taking anyone at the moment and gave me the name of the other one to call. I called the other one and told them what I was doing, and they let me stay. I paid for two days. The co-owner was Mrs. S the mother in-law. Her daughter in-law that was due any day now was the other owner. The house was very clean and comfortable. I was the only person in the house. I locked up Esmeralda under the over entrance and I went inside to wash a load of clothes. The room I was in had this huge tub in it. I filled it up and soaked in it until the water got cold. After I freshened up I walked down to a McDonalds and used that $50 gift card someone gave me a while back. On my way back I noticed a VFW lodge down this very steep hill. It looked challenging without pushing Esmeralda up it. I went straight back to the bed and breakfast. I didn't feel up to going down and drinking with the fellow Vets today. I have passed a few VFW's but I didn't stop because I felt that if I stopped I wouldn't hit my goals for the day, and I didn't have to talk about Iraq. The other owner came by the house and I got a chance to meet her. She was curious about Esmeralda out front. She was very pregnant and very nice. I got some much-needed rest and it felt good. The next few of days I got up and started my walk in the rain. It was a good day, thank God.

"God honors a beautiful blend of gift and grit! He gives the gift, and He expects us to have the grit to practice and learn how to use it effectively." Beth Moore

"Man, it's a great day to be alive"

I came to this intersection that said the road was closed seven miles down, but the locals told me that I might be able to walk around it. I thought that would be great. I also thought about getting to the seven mile mark and I am forced to turn around, which would be a 2 ½ to a 3 hour mistake, so I took the gamble and started walking. I had a choice of doing that or walking five miles or so around and out of the way. I can remember the whole time walking that day the traffic was very light which made for a nice comfortable walk. The rains continued to fall and I pushed on. I was questioning myself all the while walking that morning. "What if this, what if that," what if I cannot cross the construction area, and I would have to walk back the same way I came. There I go, thinking negative first, the way I have been conditioned all my life. And then I thought what if I can. To reassure my negative thought, I even tried to stop/flag down a few cars that whizzed past me that were coming from the direction of the bridge that was under construction, but no one would stop. I didn't get mad, I thought about what I would do if I would encounter a stranger walking along a road in the rain pushing a cart, and needing a shave. I don't think I would have stopped either. I had to make myself stop thinking about "the what if negatives," and start thinking about "the what if positives." So, I kept saying to myself, "If God will bring me to it, God will take me through it," walk by faith and not by sight. Man! I have a lot of work to do on Anthony Lee Roddy staying focused to get across America and, especially balancing that negative scale that pops up in one's life every now and then. Esmeralda and I finally made it to that mystifying construction area around and on the bridge. There were two men who appeared to be working, okayed me to walk across, even though it was closed to cars and trucks. Today was a good day, thank God.

"Man, it's a great day to be alive"

Yesterday here in Versailles after crossing that much anticipated construction area I met a guy by the name of Bob. Bob pulled up beside me as I was sucking and blowing air. I had just made it to the top of a strenuous hill attempting to get my breathing right. He shouted out, "Hey, you want something to eat?" I told him yes and we met at the top of the hill in a small church parking lot. We talked a little, but he had to get back funeral session that he was attending. He told me that I could pitch my tent in his yard if I would like. I told him that would be great. He gave me directions to get there and I arrived at his home before he made it back from the funeral. This had been a very wet day so far. I looked around his yard to find the best spot and began to set up camp. As I was setting up my tent somehow one of the support rods that hold it up snapped in half and it was starting to rain again. I'm at a point in the journey where when these things happen I don't start whining or cussing, I immediately laugh out loud and stay to myself, "count it ALL joy." I then start thinking of what supplies I have on hand and started Macgyvering something together. I found a small sleeve that I used to kind of splint the pole and I was able to put the tent up, but I knew I'd have to get another one before I reached California. Mr. Bob came home with his family and introduced me to his wife and 14 year old son. Bob had on a hat with Army embroidered on it and I asked him if he was a veteran. He said yes and told me where he did basic training. I said, "Wow, Ft. Leonard Wood, the same place I did basic training." He quickly corrected me and said, "Ft. Lost in the woods." I smiled and laughed, because anyone who has trained there used that same phrase. Bob and his family were very nice to me. His wife insisted on me staying upstairs in their extra bedroom out of the rain. The room was dry, warm and cozy which equaled a good night's sleep. The hospitality was much appreciated.

The next day she made breakfast for us and it was delicious. I got Esmeralda packed just about the time Bob and his son were headed to town to pay a bill. He offered to drive me two miles down the road past the hard dangerous parts of the route. Little does he know that this entire journey has been hard and dangerous. I told him no thanks, I'll be fine. I was standing there with my back towards Esmeralda still talking to Bob when I heard something that got my attention.

"Gratitude makes sense of our past, brings peace for today, and creates a vision for tomorrow." Melody Beattie

"Man, it's a great day to be alive"

It was the son that was car-jacking Esmeralda by trying to load her onto
the back of the truck. In doing so one side of the handle popped off and
wouldn't go back on. I can't push Esmeralda without this handle. I agreed
to a ride to the state park because I needed some time to work on the
handle. We loaded up Esmeralda while the son kept apologizing and I told
him there are worse things in life (which there are). We went to town first
and then to the park. When we got to Versailles State Park they wanted
$35.00 a night to pitch a tent. I did not want to pay that, so as we were
turning around driving out of the park we saw this road that was closed.
I asked Bob to stop, and I told him I will get off here. We moved the road
block barriers and drove down it and I found a good spot. We downloaded
Esmeralda and I gave him the cash I had in my pocket, which was $27.00.
He told me it was enough to get some supplies on their way back through
town, and thanked me. I found a spot that looked almost perfect, but as I
did my walk around the area I noticed what looked like bear clawing marks
on a couple of trees up high on the trunk. I went to a different location
further down the road. I found a better spot off the road where I could view
passersby and not be noticed. The next morning as I was getting packed
up, I heard some very loud talking ladies walking down this closed road.
They were gossiping about someone they both knew. It seemed to me that
they were exercising because they were walking at a brisk pace. I sat there
very quiet and still and even slinked down like a fawn camouflaged in the
bush waiting on the mother. They passed and their voices slowly faded in
the distance. Following not far behind was this man who was walking a
large sized black poodle. The dog knew I was in the bush and let out a
non-aggressive bark towards my direction. I made myself motionless and
the man pulled the dog on. The two women and the man walking the dog
eventually made their way back, passing my camp. The women walked past

me oblivious of me sitting there watching them. They just kept on gabbing negatively about this person they both knew. The man who was walking the dog was a different story. As they got closer the dog started barking aggressively this time passing, and the man kept asking the dog, "what da see, boy, what da see?"

"Is the glass half full, or half empty? It depends on whether you're pouring or drinking." Bill Cosby

"Man, it's a great day to be alive"

I got to thinking if the man lets his dog off the leash its coming straight for me, so I decided to make it a point for him to see me. I loudly cleared my throat and stood up. Once I was up, I said in a loud professional clear friendly voice, "Good Morning, Sir," and then let him know what I was doing. The gentleman seemed okay with what I told him and wished me well as he walked on. I was packing up Esmeralda anyway to start my exit out of the park. If this gentleman wanted to tell someone that I was back here, I had to be on my way if someone happens to come. My main concern was to make it to California before Christmas. The rest I had gotten was much needed and appreciated; besides I was eager to get started. When taking down my tent I immediately started thinking of ways I could fix it. There was no procrastination on this journey, because I had the burning desire to make it to California before Christmas. I found something that I could use in my tools that Dad told me to take. Dad would tell me as I was packing Esmeralda before this journey, *"It's better to have and not want, than to want and not have."* I took everything. Believe me that philosophy worked the entire journey. I pulled out my phone and ordered a new tent because I could see that I had a good phone signal. I had it shipped to a cousin's house here in the northern part of Indiana. My cousin Angela was okay with it coming to her house and would bring it out to me once it arrived. Today was a good day thank God.

"Good, better, best. Never let it rest. 'Til your good is better and your better is best." St. Jerome

"Man, it's a great day to be alive"

The next day started out with an overcast sky and then it started to lightly rain. After about halfway into the walk the sun came out which gave me traction mentally to push me down the road even faster. With four hours under my belt it started to rain again, and this time very hard. It was coming down so hard it was getting very dangerous to walk. The pounding rain had the visibility level very, very short, (zero). I thought if I'm having a hard time seeing cars, the people in their 3,000 pound vehicles would have a hard time seeing me. I found a spot right off the side of the road. With the rain coming down so hard the spot that I chose didn't feel the most conspicuous. I started setting up my tent anyway. I cut a few tree branches and some of the shrubs to camouflage Esmeralda and me. I finally made it inside my tent, and it felt good. Now the aerobics class begins. I have to get out of the wet clothes and put on something dry in a one-person tent. After that I would always hang my socks thinking they would be dry enough to wear the next dry. Sometimes yes and sometimes no, I count this ALL joy. Today was a good day thank God.

Man, it's a great day to be alive"

I did some homework this morning while lying in my sleeping bag by looking at my walkabout route for the day. I set a goal of 23 miles which would bring me to a town called Seymour. The rain had stopped, and I had to do my morning constitutional. As I unzipped the tent, I could see that I was not as camouflaged and concealed as I thought. I was pretty visible, but nevertheless I had to find a spot. So, as I timed the traffic that zoomed by for a long enough gap, I would dart off into the bushes past Esmeralda and handle my business. While looking at the map this morning I realized that I was halfway through Indiana (hallelujah). I ate some breakfast, put on those damp socks from yesterday and broke down camp. I had also found a place to sleep for the night in the town 23 miles away. The motel in Seymour wasn't on the main strip so I had to go through one of the neighborhoods. After making it to the motel, which had about eight rooms with a small laundry room to wash clothes, it was a good feeling. The manager was very polite and seemed to be empathetic to my cause and what I had done up to this point. I asked if he knew where I could order a pizza. The gentleman told me of a place and that they did not have delivery. He said that he would drive over and pick it up for me. I thought that was very kind of him to do that. He came back with two pizzas for the price of one. The laundry that I had started earlier was finished now. All I had to do for the night was to hunker down in my room, rest my feet, and watch a little TV. The pizza was very good, and I washed every bite down with some ice cold milk. Whenever I would order a pizza from anywhere during this journey I would always put in a request for some milk. The person taking down my order would always repeat milk, surprisingly.

"Be kind whenever possible. It is always possible." Dalai Lama

"Man, it's a great day to be alive"

I was gorging myself with that pizza like a bear getting ready for its hibernation season, and to replenish the protein and strength I so badly needed. The night was getting late and I was beginning to drift into the dream state of mind when the phone rang and scared the heebie-jeebies out of me. It was the manager at the front desk. He wanted to know if I was willing to meet with a local newspaper reporter and tell my story tomorrow. I said yes and the reporter would be there in the morning before I left. Man, it's been some good and kind hearted people from Maine up until this very point here in Indiana, all seven states so far. Today was a good day thank God.

"Man, it's a great day to be alive"

Today's walk going through Brownstown, Indiana this young man stopped alongside me in his car. He shouted out the passenger side window "Hey, my name's Richard and I'm the local newspaper reporter." He wanted to know if he could talk with me. He was a very polite young man during our interview. The reporter asked the basic five questions, how many miles are you walking, where did you sleep, how many pair of shoes have I gone through, how many miles a day you walked, and what's my cause. I'd tell them my cause, the Make-A-Wish foundation and I usually get one of two responses. They would say, "Oh, the Make-A-Wish foundation, the children," or they would say, "I know someone who has been gifted a wish with their family." The young man and I stood there and talked alongside the road for a little while, and I then pushed on. The walk today has been good, despite the fact that I could see this huge dark grey cloud in the distance. That was not a pretty sight. Looking down at my cell phone that just lit up, it was a text from a family I befriended while staying at their bed and breakfast. It was Ms. Sharon letting me know that her daughter-in-law Natasha had the baby. Thank God that was great news for the day and it made me feel good with a smile. Then my phone went off again, but this time it was beeping and honking like a loud tropical bird. It was the National Weather Service report alert telling me there's been a tornado spotted in the county. Things around me along with the wind, started to speed up and right along with it I started walking faster, I was thinking I don't have any place to go. Where am I walking so fast too? These dark ominous clouds were starting to gather overhead, it looked pretty serious. Then a police officer pulled alongside me with his lights on. With the wind blowing and the atmosphere mixing up all those excited molecules, things are moving fast. The police officer was telling me to take cover because of a storm approaching. He asked me where I was going and I told him California. The police officer's response was, you have to get through this first, take cover down over there. It was some type of business down there, though I couldn't make out what type of business it was. The officer saluted me and then quickly pulled off.

"I'm starting to think this world is just a place for us to learn that we need each other more than we want to admit."— Richelle E. Goodrich, Smile Anyway

"Man, it's a great day to be alive"

As I got closer to the business I could see a lady out front waving me to come over. It was a veterinarian doctor's office. The lady introduced herself and said that I could park Esmeralda around back. She went through the office to the back to let the garage door up. I now could get Esmeralda and park her in the garage out of the approaching storm. Dr. Joyce introduced me to the other employees and told them what I was doing; they were curious about my journey across America and shot out question after question. I told them if I could sit down and take a look at my feet, which had some pretty wicked blisters on them, we could talk. We sat and talked while I doctored on my feet. The storm seemed to miss us and roll on. Thank God

Esmeralda and I took off for Starve Hollow State Park with my feet feeling a little uncomfortable. Then my feet got a lot uncomfortable and I was in some pain, to a point where I started limping. With the rain it's been getting my foot bottoms nice and tender and my socks were not completely dry when I put them on this morning. Esmeralda and I finally made it to the park. That night at the park the groundskeepers and security were telling the residents to take cover in the shower house tonight if needed. That bad weather that bypassed us earlier was swinging around later tonight. I took off the helmet that'd been riding on top of Esmeralda the whole way, and placed it in the tent just in case I needed it. About 1:30 a.m. the wind was blowing so hard that it woke me up. At that time, I put the helmet on my head. I literally had to grab the support frame of the tent to keep the winds from taking it. As I sat there with this helmet on clinching the poles inside the tent, and praying that no widow maker trees would fall my way. It was a terrifying moment. I thought about what the security person said earlier that day about going to the shower house, but I wasn't going to leave that warm dry tent, so I rode it out.

The next morning, I could see that the high tornado winds had caused widespread devastation with tree branches everywhere, and some of them were huge. I thank God and the power of prayer for me having a safe night. As I kind of picked up the branches around my tent I could see in the distance a group of men walking towards my area. They were from the correctional facility walking through the campground picking up the fallen branches from the high winds last night. I had a chance to talk with them a little bit. They were curious about Esmeralda and I told them the story about why I was walking across America. The next day my cousin Angela came with the new tent and I continued through Indiana with the quote, "Go west young man" playing over and over in my head.

With the state line in my crosshairs, Esmeralda and I were making great time and will be in the land of Lincoln before dark.

"Take responsibility of your own happiness, never put it in other people's hands." — Roy T. Bennett

What Indiana means to me

Indiana Indiana, what you mean to me
With rolling grass hills as far as you can see
Indiana Indiana, Lincoln's boyhood home
Along these long country roads
I walked miles alone
Soybeans in one patch and corn in the next
I always thought of basketball
In this Hoosiers nest
Indiana's hospitality has exceeded most
From sleeping in backyards to being the host
The people here have been friendly and kind
With laughter and smiles
Which is always a good sign
Indiana Hoosiers has been a great state
But I must keep on trucking
To meet my date

Chapter 8

Illinois

"Man, it's a great day to be alive"

Finally I made it to my birth state, the land of Lincoln (ILLINOIS). I had entered Mt. Carmel, Illinois. But before I actually crossed the Illinois state line, I could see a gray truck that looked like my parents' vehicle. I was walking with traffic entering Mt. Carmel to make time that day and get to a motel room in Illinois before dark. This gray truck reached me, but it was in the opposite lane going past honking the horn in a friendly way. I didn't think anything of it (just another by-passer acknowledging my walking) so I threw up my hand to say hey, and thank you. Then the truck turned around and pulled in front of me and these two crazy screaming ladies jumped out. By this time, I could see that it was my sisters. I did not expect to see them here. They were jumping, screaming and crying with happiness to see me. I had made it to the 8th state of this journey, and it felt good. My sisters' reason for being there was twofold. First was to see how I was doing and secondly to pick me up for our mother's birthday party they were planning the next day. We stood there with this joyful reunion hugging and talking on the side of the road. I told them to meet me right past the state welcoming sign which was less than a mile away. I made it to the state sign of Illinois. I did my usual selfies poses in front of the sign with the happiness of accomplishing an interesting feat. I said to myself I had done it. I have walked through Indiana, President Lincoln's boyhood home. I have just walked to Illinois, President Lincoln's adulthood home, and now my sisters are driving me to Kentucky (the Chitlin Circuit), President Lincoln's childhood home. I think that's pretty cool. My sisters agreed to bring me back to this Illinois starting point when the party was over. I ended up staying one week in Paducah, Kentucky waiting on my sister to have an off day to take me back to the point where they picked me up from. The week off from walking allowed me to refresh my batteries physically. It allowed me to hang out with Mom and Dad as I did much needed repairs to Esmeralda. While in Paducah, Esmeralda and I attended a Black History parade and got our picture in the local view magazine. It wasn't planned, but I think it was a great way to spend some down time and have some fun with the family. Esmeralda and I stayed our welcome in the unbridled state of Kentucky and eventually made our way back over to the Illinois side to continue the journey. My sisters, Mom and Dad took me back to Illinois to a state park and dropped me off. I could see that the park had a lot of raccoons. When we stopped and downloaded Esmeralda off the truck, I was happy to be getting back on the road again.

"When you realize who the good people are in your life, you're so lucky."
Sophia Bush

"Man, it's a great day to be alive"

I could see that dusk was falling as rapid as a star during its downward descent through the sky. Night was falling and some nocturnal activity starting to happen. What I mean is that I could see some of raccoons moving around. It was like they were sizing me up. I got my tent up and walked back to where Mom and Dad were sitting in the truck to say good-bye. As I got somewhat close to the truck, my dad says as he was pointing, "Hey, that raccoon is going towards your tent." I turned around and ran it off. Dad and Mom came out of the truck as we quickly prayed and they took off.

"Man, it's a great day to be alive"

"I got settled in and went to sleep for the night. All through the night I could hear raccoons outside my tent trying to get inside Esmeralda, I thought. I would make a loud noise inside my tent and they would stop momentarily and start again. I would keep saying to myself Esmeralda is all buttoned and zipped down. She should be safe. She was not safe. The raccoons went through the back of Esmeralda like she was some road kill on the side of the road. They had bags scattered all over this side of the camping site. After my policing the area I made some breakfast, but couldn't find those six hardboiled eggs my sister gave me. I thought I must have left them in the truck, oh well. That evening when I spoke to my dad he looked through his truck and there were no eggs. The crafty raccoons with those five long tapered fingers stole my six hardboiled eggs that I was so looking forward to eating. Oh well, count it ALL joy.

"My brethren, count it all joy when you fall into various trials, knowing that the testing of your faith produces patience." James 1:2-3

"Man, it's a great day to be alive"

I finally made it out of the park and was headed towards a hotel to get a room for the night. The room was a day's walk from my birth town in Illinois. The town is Pulaski, Illinois, population 350 people. This Walkabout America trek is very significant to me going through Illinois. The significance that's so dear to me is the fact that I'm walking to my birthplace. My mother gave birth to me in a house back in 1959 on this plot of grounds. I made it to the hotel and got a room for the night. I ordered a pizza drank some Mellow Yellow out of a liter bottle and ate like a king. The next morning while walking down Rt. 51 I ran into my Uncle Joe's older brother James and Janice Tucker. They stopped on the side of the road and I had a chance to talk to them. That felt good connecting with someone my parents grew up with. They were rooting for me to make it California.

I made it to my birthplace. The house had been demolished years ago. The young kids who were hanging around under the shade tree I didn't recognize. I think I'm going to hang on to the memories when I used to run these little dirt roads pushing a tire full of rocks barefooted with the rest of the little rascals. As I can remember the time back then seem so easier with our families living in poverty. We didn't know any difference, we just accepted our environment.

I pushed on to Mounds, Illinois where my cousin the town's mortician had a gathering waiting on me to feed and cheer me on and talk about the Walkabout-America. After the festivities, Esmeralda and I took a 20-mile ride across the Ohio/Mississippi River to Charleston, Missouri., with a friend of my sister, Mr. Sug. He was a blessing to have a flat trailer for Esmeralda to ride on.

Anthony "Silverback" Roddy

<u>What Illinois means to me</u>
Illinois is good
Illinois is great
It is considered to be my birth state
With soybeans gone and cornfields here
This state gives me absolutely no fear
The soil is rich and the soil is black
I have 10,000 reasons to come back
With the mission at hand
And attitudes high
It's time to exit this state and say
Good bye

Chapter 9

Missouri

"Man, it's a great day to be alive"

Mr. Sug and I made it across the river into Charleston, Missouri. He took me to his home where he and his wife feed me and gave me a place to stay for the night. I am forever grateful for that. The next morning Esmeralda and I took off going west with a Ziplock bag full of home-grown cherry tomatoes. As I walked about 10 minutes from Sug's house a little boy around 10 maybe 12 years old approached me on a small bicycle. Esmeralda and I didn't stop I was walking at a good clip. We were having a conversation with the young man about him and what I was doing. His main focus as we were talking was on my Pop Tarts lying on top of Esmeralda. He would answer a question and immediately without putting a period at the end ask about the Pop Tarts. I told him I would give him the whole package of two if he could tell me what it means to him when he hears the word "colored." He answered, "YOU FOOL, we both colored." I did an Eyes Right, (still walking at a good pace) and looked at the boy and started laughing so hard that I couldn't stop laughing, as I agreed with him. The little boy even started laughing. I gave him the Pop Tarts and told him to tell his mother that we met, and I told him to be safe. The young boy headed east on his little jumping bike. He had one hand on his handlebar and with the other hand he was cramming one of those Pop Tarts in his mouth like Cookie Monster on Sesame Street. It reminded me of a Norman Rockwell painting. He was a very interesting young lad. Today was a good day, thank God.

I have noticed the demographics in some of the areas that I've traveled. The Charleston / Sikeston, area so far on this trip has contained the most Black population that I have seen, while trekking across this magnificent country. That's just my observation. The next day I had a pretty nice walk. There was nothing hurting me that day, thank God. As I walked

238

mile marker after mile marker, I was somewhere out in the Mark Twain National Forest area when I saw this pilot. He was flying by me doing what crop-duster pilots do. As I was fumbling around attempting to take a photo of him, he buzzed by me as if he was showing off. He would fly sideways between things which I thought was so cool, and under wires. I even said to myself, "Man, all these different things that I'm experiencing just by walking" (that's Crazy). I would like to thank God as much as I can, because without God's Spirit I have no faith. No faith, I have no health. No health equals No walk.

I finally made it to a campground and settled in. During my trek that day I befriended a passer-by driving out of a Dairy Queen. As I was walking out the parking lot entrance there was the lady who was parallel to me in a Sport Utility Vehicle and with her window down. She asked me what I was doing. I thought that she was kinda flirty, and I didn't back down.

"Man, it's a great day to be alive"

She insisted that I take some cash she was handing out the window of her SUV and I said no, go online and give it to the Make-A-Wish children. She persistently insisted again that I take the money and buy me some food and that she would give to the Make-A-Wish children also. I gave her one of my cards with my Go Fund Me page information and with my phone number. I could feel our chemistry through our reactions toward each other. Maybe I was reading too much into it. She then drove away. About an hour later she found me, asked me to stop, and had a couple bottles of water for me. She had pulled her SUV in front of me and Esmeralda. I don't think Esmeralda was too keen on what this lady was doing. She got out of her SUV and we talked more on side the road. The conversation was very easy, comfortable, and funny. She told me she liked my calf muscles and had noticed them before I met her at the Dairy Queen. If we dated while I'm walking, fine, if we don't get together while I'm walking, that's fine too. I may never see this lady again, she'll just have a story like me. I didn't think I would ever see this lady again, so what do I have to lose by censoring what we're talking about. She told me she looked me up on the internet and read my story and started crying. A story that she thought was amazing by helping the children. After our conversation I told her the next town I would be staying in and she gave me her phone number. This young lady and I would text one another all the way to Arizona. With all this walking it had me with great blood pressure, and I could tell. The next few days I made it down to a small campsite near Diamond, Missouri. The man that was in the office charged me 30 dollars to stay. I was there for three days. On the 2nd day there was a blonde headed lady on a golf cart who came down to where I had my tent pitched and handed me an envelope. She was the owner. She said that she and her husband looked me up on the internet and read about what I was doing and decided to give me the 30 dollars back. She even thanked me for being a veteran. I thought that was the nicest thing that happened to me that day. Man, God's good.

"It's not that diamonds are a girl's best friend, but it's your best friends who are your diamonds." Gina Barreca

"Man, it's a great day to be alive"

There was this older gentleman and his wife that were from Texas. They were curious about what I was doing. The couple came over to talk to me more than once. They became good camping buddies. The next morning, they invited me to their RV for breakfast and asked if I had clothes to wash. They had a very nice RV with a small compact car in tow. I made it to their RV with dirty clothes in a drawstring laundry bag over my back (looking like a dirty Santa). They served me fried grits, fried eggs, a couple slabs of fried bacon, some homemade biscuits with strawberry jelly, a glass of milk, and some orange juice. I was down with everything except the fried grits. I ate them but fried grits, I'm a Yankee from the North; I grew up eating warm Cream-of-Wheat looking grits with sugar and butter. I really appreciated that breakfast, it hit the spot. As we sat there and talked they asked if I wanted to go to Diamond, Missouri to visit the George Washington Carver museum with them. I accepted the invitation and rolled with them. Walking the grounds of the museum gave me this feeling of accomplishment. I thought finally I have been given the honor of being able to walk the grounds of my all-time great inventors/humanitarians. The couple that I was with I thought went above and beyond with their hostility. They bought me some lunch at the place and then purchased me a shirt. As I walked the property of the young man who would be called the plant doctor, I could see how nature could influence the young inquisitive mind of George Washington Carver. Nature was a huge factor into making George who he was. The next day I went around the campground and bid my farewell with the ones that I knew and headed west.

As I walked, about an hour and a half into the walk the lady that owned the campground pulled up behind me and Esmeralda blowing her horn.

I stopped and put the park brake on Esmeralda to walk back to her car. By this time, she had gotten out of the car and was walking towards me. She handed me a 50-dollar bill, gave me a tight bear hug and wished me the best. I was very grateful for the money and the love and used it on supplies. I could smell her as I walked for at least 10 miles that day from that great bear hug she gave me. As I mentioned earlier, I had my aiming sights on Oklahoma and was getting closer and closer with every step. The walk that day was dry, comfortable and this last leg of the road leading into Oklahoma was nice level and smooth with fresh pavement. I felt a very easy calmness as I walked into this new state. Missouri had been a very interesting walk. I had seen some things I wouldn't have seen anywhere else in the world. I think leaving Missouri would be a huge milestone on the journey, meaning that I'm at or a little over the halfway mark. The calmness and self-worth are from the fact I have completed over half of this journey.

"You've got to be strong enough for love. It's very easy to be cool and cynical. It's very difficult to just let yourself go and be in love. You've got to be strong enough for that." **Noel Gallagher**

<u>*What Missouri means to me*</u>
Missouri Missouri, the Show Me state
I walked through some areas I thought
Were great.
Mother of the West
And the largest beer brewery in the world
The arch goes way up
Before it makes its big curl.
Missouri and the South Ozarks
Takes you along
Mark Twain National Park.
From Langston Hughes
to
Walter Cronkite
Missouri natives have lived a great site
It's time to go and I have to
Run
There were times in this state I had some fun

Chapter 10

Oklahoma

"Man, it's a great day to be alive"

As I'm entering into another state it's a little exciting. About 5 to 10 miles before crossing the state line, I would usually see the other state's license plates going to and from the different states. I always welcomed the site of new state license plates because after looking at one state license plate on the back of cars and trucks as they go by gets a little redundant after 25 to 30 days. So, I welcome the new state plates when I see them. I finally made it to OKLAHOMA, which has the largest American Indian population of any state and it's going to be my longest state to walk across because I'm going across the Panhandle. After I did my traditional selfie in front of the state sign, I looked up a campground on my phone that was 12 miles out. While walking to the campsite passing the entrance of the first Oklahoma casino that; I had come across, the energy was bustling with activity. I was really tempted to walk over and try to get a place to stay for the night, but I knew I had not walked enough to rest for the day to hit my goal. The energy that radiated from those casino doors when they opened made me think that I should be a part of that excitement. You know, the more I thought about it, the more I didn't want to exhaust the energy doing that, but I can use the energy for walking. I finally made it to the so-called campground. It looked to be a small area with a few acres that was tucked away around the bend in the road. But there was a problem, the front gate was closed and locked. To the right of the locked gate there was this sign nailed to the tree and it said "WARNING: Forget the dog, beware of the owner," this was with a picture sign of a hand holding a pistol pointing at me.

"Never give up on what you really want to do. The person with big dreams is more powerful than the one with all the facts." H. Jackson Brown, Jr.

"Man, it's a great day to be alive"

I thought to myself NOOOOOO! Then I shouted to myself NOOOOOOOOO! I've been walking all day and it was getting late. I stood there thinking what to do next. I looked around trying to find a reasonable area to go to. I kept looking at that poster sign on that tree and thinking how I can best use my options. I thought to myself again, "Well, if I go past this gate and this sign I've got to be on edge the whole night until I leave the next morning" and then just like that I thought of Spike Lee's movie (Do The Right Thing) and said no, don't do it, Tony. I picked up my phone and gripped it as though I was choking it (awwww). With my lips seized together, I grunted and blamed the phone for guiding us here. Heck, it got me here and didn't say that this place was closed. I had to think positive and get out of here. I took another look around and could see in the distance that there was a small area butted up against the wood line (which I would explore later) that would work for the night. I could see that the county highway department had been doing some road repairs. There was a small piece of road no longer than 40 feet that ran off the main drag that led to nowhere. I had to go down there using that piece of dead-end road. It was a smooth walk leading up to this closed campsite. I turned Esmeralda around and headed for that little wooded area. The area had sod that was recently laid which I thought would be great for pitching my tent. Wrong! The sod was laid over some small medium rocks and some of the rocks were as big as cantaloupes which were really hard to drive my tent stakes into the ground around them. This rock and sod must have been some overage material that they put in this area. I got camp set up, ate and got into my sleeping bag. As I'm lying there, I'm thinking this is my first bed of rocks to sleep on (like I'm planning on doing this again). That was not a very comfortable night. It gives a new meaning to the phrase "I slept like a rock." Morning came and I decided not to walk that day and do some repairs on Esmeralda. I pulled Esmeralda onto that dead-end piece of road and put the spare wheel on. The wheel I replaced was a soft wheelchair wheel and I was putting on a hard rubber wheelchair wheel. I'd been ignorant to the fact of knowing all wheelchair wheels are not the same hard material consistency, and the different sizes. I apologize for that, but now I know. Walking through Oklahoma was by far the longest state I had to cross to get to California thus far. It actually took me around 43 days to make it all the way through Oklahoma and it is obvious westward Panhandle above Texas. I was really getting tired of looking at Oklahoma's state driver's license plates day after day. I always started to get excited when I would see the next state's driver's license plate on cars that would appear periodically crossing over into another state whether for work or traveling. It was like a sense of accomplishment and I would know I was hitting my goals.

"I think goals should never be easy, they should force you to work, even if they are uncomfortable at the time." --------Michael Phelps

"Man, it's a great day to be alive"

There were some days walking through the Panhandle where I could only walk a measly seven miles maximum, or four miles at the minimum. The crosswinds and the northwestern winds determined whether I was going to hit my 20-mile mark for the day or not. Some of the trees in this area had grown in the direction of the wind blowing. While doing the Walkabout-America I had plenty of time to think and observe the world around me. This one particular day while walking the Panhandle I came up on this orange and black construction sign which read "Road work in 1,000 feet." I said to myself, "I wonder how many big strides it would take for me to walk 1,000 feet?" At this point on this Walkabout-America I had acquired a pretty large gape for covering miles quickly. It took me 415 large strides (which my strides were around 2.5 to 3 feet with every huge step) depending on how fast I would walk, to cover a thousand feet. My mind was wandering one day while clipping down the Panhandle and I looked over at the telephone poles that lined the narrow country road. I told myself that I must get through Oklahoma quicker, so I come up with a plan to run with Esmerelda. With every 415th stride (1000ft) I would run three telephone poles with Esmeralda's heavy girth and stop. I would then walk another 415 strides (1,000ft) which equaled about five telephone poles and run another three telephone poles. This went on from mile after mile until I reached Boise City. At the hotel in Boise City, I had a chance to meet two young men from Switzerland who took me to lunch. One of the young men was 19 years old and his older brother was 21 years old. They were on their way to Yellowstone National Park in Wyoming. They were curious about what I was doing, and I was curious about what they were doing. I asked them if they lived here and they said no. They were here in the United States temporarily working on a ranch in Texas. The owner let them borrow one of his flatbed pick-up trucks to drive to Yellowstone National

Park, which I thought was great for them. Even though I was doing great things for the Make-A-Wish kids, these two young men inspired me. It made me think of what I was doing at their age, and where I would have been back then. Oddly enough I was in Europe (Germany) at their age being "All That I Could Be" in the Army. After I told them my story, they said that I inspired them. There you have it, two people who inspire one another can achieve great riches in life physically and mentally. They were living their dream. I then told them how that I was 20 years of age when I was over in Germany "Being All That I Could Be in the Army". I told them how I was living my dream while in Europe at age 20/21 and living my dream today in Oklahoma. The Panhandle was no joke and I hit my goal on my 43rd day in Oklahoma. Thanks be to God and the wonderful inspiring people God has placed into my life on this journey. Today was a good day, thank God.

"If you don't think every day is a good day, just try missing one." Cavett Robert

<u>*What Oklahoma means to me*</u>
Oklahoma Oklahoma, the 46th state
with
Bison in the plain
And Garth Brooks in the fame
Osage, Caddo, Kiowa, Comanche and Wichita
Are all tribes of people along the way that I saw,
With Oklahoma's neck as long as it could be
Walking in 28 mph winds was truly a
A sight to see
With Oklahoma's flag flying green, brown, and blue
Walking across this state will eventually tire you
The 43 days looking at Oklahoma license plates
I was ready to enter another state
Good-bye, Oklahoma, it's been fun
But I must keep pushing to beat the sun

Chapter 11

New Mexico

"Man, it's a good day to be alive"

At last I made it to New Mexico, my place of residency. I had pictured in my mind what it would be like crossing into New Mexico even before I crossed the state line. The homecoming was exactly like I'd imagined and even more. I found a place to sleep for the night here in Clayton at the Hotel Eklund. This hotel is on the National Registry of Historic places and legend has it there's a ghost by the name of Black Jack Ketchum that haunts the place. The lady at the hotel's guest registry seemed very nice and friendly. I got a good vibe the minute I walked into the lobby. This is part of the philosophy of what I expect of myself (which is good) and in doing so it reflected back to me from others (most of the time). If I'm happy for life and friendly I expect that in return, like a contagious happiness just the opposite of a contagious disease, but just the same as they're both contagious; you choose your destiny. I asked the lady at the front desk if she would sponsor me a room and she asked me to wait a minute as she went to find the co-owner and they both said yes and they'd feed me for free also.

The Hotel Eklund in Clayton, is a great remnant of the past. The authentic saloon/eating area still have a few bullet holes in the ceiling from shootouts long ago. As I walked the little towns that were closer to Colorado, I would see signs telling me I'm entering "The Rocky Mountains". When I first saw a sign that said, "You are now entering The Rocky Mountains" it gave me a reality check kind of feeling. I'm thinking to myself, there's no turning back now. Reading that sign pushed my fear button a little bit also, because it's late October and I am thinking I must change my route. My original route was taking me to the four corners (NM, CO, UT, AZ) and continuing through Utah, Nevada, and then California to the city by the beach, Monterey. The image that kept popping up in my brain was that of an old Western movie with the cowboys suffering through a winter somewhere in Nevada, so I decided that I didn't want to walk that route anymore. As I'm making a 12,441feet push up Baldy Mountain, it's taking me through a scenic part of the Carson National Forest. The whole time I'm thinking Southern Arizona and then cutting across Southern California to San Diego. This route would keep me warmer.

"Life is full of surprises, why is that always surprising?" Cathleen Shine

"Man, it's a great day to be alive"

As I pushed further up the mountain it was taking me to a town called Eagle Nest. It was there that I was invited to speak to some elementary school students that later put me in their school yearbook. They not only put me in their yearbook, they gave me a two-page spread. It is a blessing to know that God shows up everywhere we walk if we take the time to recognize it. I will be a permeant fixture with that school forever. The town of Eagle Nest by far is the most beautiful place I have stayed since I've been on this journey. I have envisioned a lot of places along this trip that I wanted to take up residency in, but this place is my favorite. I finally made it to Cimarron Canyon State Park headed to Eagle Nest. It's November and I had to stay extremely careful to watch for possible danger or difficulties, which I know I'm going to run into. I have come too far to stop, and still two more states to conquer. As I set up camp in the Cimarron Canyon state park, there was another reminder to let me know that I was not at the top of the food chain. There were these bear food lockers that the bears can't get into. I had to walk down to them and store my goods away from my tent. After eating dinner I took everything that could be used as food that I think the bears would eat, even my toothpaste down and locked it up for the night. It reminded me of the times going to play racket ball or something, when I just locked my stuff up in the locker and would get it a few hours later. I had been thinking about changing my route for the last few weeks, so that I could walk into the warmth for these winter months remaining.

The next morning while eating something for breakfast I made a decision to go south. I will be walking to Arizona going south down to Phoenix. After Phoenix, go west across the Baja sand dunes to Imperial Beach, California, the most southern town in California bordering Tijuana, Mexico. I finally made it to Eagle Nest. After making several stops pushing Esmeralda up this hill I got to the top and it was spectacular. There was this huge lake at the very top, "Eagle Nest Lake State Park". It was like a National Geographic scene, I saw a few deer scatter in the distance as they ran along the water. It was amazing. I could see that there was a hotel just as you entered the town and I said to myself that I would bypass this one and hope to see another one, and if not, walk back. I have noticed that there is always a hotel at the end of leaving town throughout my walk. There were four more hotels once I got past the first one. I eventually ended up staying at the Laguna Vista Lodge. The owner was a veteran, which helped me out tremendously. I stayed there a few days until my son brought up the granddaughters from Albuquerque. The owner was very accommodating in helping me stay comfortable.

"We don't realize that somewhere within us all, there does exist a supreme self who is eternally at peace." Elizabeth Gilbert

"Man, it's a great day to be alive"

I made it to Taos, New Mexico and walking over the Gorge. Wow, this bridge is very intimidating. It has 911 phones on the bridge; I'm thinking it's to give people that want to commit suicide a chance to talk to someone. I could see into the rocks below way down deep there was a car all crumbled up. I couldn't make out what type it was, but it was white. It looked like somebody ran that car over the rocky cliff and committed suicide. After crossing the bridge not far from the gorge I could see a community of houses that were off the grid and some of them looked decent. The stride I kept was one of an Olympic fast walker going for the gold or me just trying to make it to California before Christmas. I made it around the other side of the gorge where there was no bridge or people. I decided to set up camp about twenty feet from the edge of the gorge so that I could wake up the next morning while brushing my teeth and spit down the long descent and watch the toothpaste vanish before my eyes. The gorge looks like a part of the Grand Canyon, deep, scary, dangerous, and beautiful to me. As I walked over to the edge to look down, I felt a little fear kick in because I thought to myself this would be a terrible way to die falling off the edge of this cliff. I keep looking around thinking and hoping no one would push me off, so I got down and laid on my belly to low crawl to the edge to look down and take some pictures. There was no one there but me and the murder of crows flying overhead.

Taos, New Mexico was a great place to visit but I must keep pushing southwest to Gallup, which butts up against Arizona. The weather here in the great Southwest was starting to change for the worst. Once making it to Gallup in the four corners region and with it being late October along with the elevation, I woke up to about three or four inches of snow on top of Esmeralda this morning. I had Esmeralda tied up (locked up outside) like a horse and she wasn't happy about it. Gallup is midway between Albuquerque, New Mexico and Flagstaff, Arizona. It is also dissected by the historical Route 66 which runs through Albuquerque.

"Success is a journey, not a destination." Ben Sweetland.

"Man, it's a great day to be alive"

I left Gallup "The Heart of Indian Country" and continued down Route 602 towards the Zuni Pueblo area. My goal today was to get out of the state of New Mexico. Today was a good day to walk and the Southwest looked so beautiful and rugged. The roads were flat and even, which allowed me to cover a lot of ground. Midway through the walk that day I could see a young lady jogging up ahead with a puppy (German Shepherd mix) about four months old. Throughout the walk so far, whenever I'd encounter somebody running, jogging or walking I'd set a goal to catch them before they made it to a certain object that I had visually marked on the side of the road. In doing this I'm pulled down the road that much faster with that energy. If I miss my goal in catching up to them, I reset the goal and find different visual marks, but I always catch up to them. As I kept creeping closer to them, the young lady's puppy was looking behind him at me and trying to run at the same time.

The young lady would occasionally stop to encourage the puppy to keep following her. I could see as I got closer to them that the young lady was pregnant. I thought, wow! She reminded me of Hiawatha. I was in Native America country near the Zuni Reservation. I finally reached them and now she stopped and said, "You walk pretty fast," and then she wanted to know what I was doing. I told her the what, when, where, and how and then she told me a little bit about her life. Our conversation on the side of the road was very comfortable and warm. The young lady said that I was inspirational, and I told her that God is blessing me with the gift to communicate with others. She told me that she had just finished school to be a registered nurse with a specialty in Pediatrics. The puppy finally warmed up to me and let me rub his head. The young lady also mentioned that after she has the baby she would be moving to Albuquerque. We finished our conversation and she crossed over to the other side of the road to head back to her home. As I pulled off going west to the Arizona state line I couldn't help but to think how that young lady just inspired me to keep pushing.

"Make your life a masterpiece, imagine no limitations on what you can be, have, or do." Brian Tracy

<u>What New Mexico means to me</u>
New Mexico, New Mexico
The great southwest
With tumbleweeds and dry weather
It is the best.
Road Runners and coyotes
They roam the land
With rattle snakes and Gila monsters
Crawling in the sand
The state is beautiful which I must cleave
With snow and cold weather
It's time to leave

Chapter 12

Arizona

"Man, it's a great day to be alive"

Today was a long and hard walk but, nevertheless I had hit my goal today by entering Arizona. As I made my way to a rest stop that's off of Interstate 40, my right heal was really blistered up to the point where it was bleeding. It was really hurting me to walk the last few miles before stopping for the day. After making it to the rest stop I did some first aid on my bleeding heel and ate some dinner. I was in no condition to walk a few more miles before completely shutting down for the day. I knew I couldn't set up camp in the rest area without attracting a state trooper. While sitting there I said a prayer in my head, "God, give me the faith to know that someone will help me." As I sat there watching people drive in and out there was this one couple that was walking around stretching that wanted to know what I was doing. They also wanted to know about Esmeralda. The lady looked down at my one foot with the sock off and asked if they could help. I said, "Hallelujah, God is good."

The lady smiled and said, "Yes, every day."

I told them I could not walk another mile because I need to rest this one foot and I could not camp here. I needed a ride nine miles to the next town, Sanders, Arizona. The lady was doing all the talking, the husband was quiet; he was probably trying to figure me out. She said, "Sure! We have to go to Chambers to visit some folks and Sanders is just before it."

The husband and I loaded Esmeralda in the back of his pickup truck and they gave me a ride. I left $30.00 in the back seat before I got out because they wouldn't take it from me. There are good people everywhere in the world. I had to walk another few miles after they dropped me off to get out of town (and that was very painful) to find a camping spot.

At last, I found refuge in the back of a small church right outside of town. It was an almost perfect spot. I went back to cover up my tracks in the sand like they did in the Western movies with a broken branch off a tree. I used the branch and walked backward to cover up my tracks.

"Create the highest, grandest vision possible for your life. Because you become what you believe." Oprah Winfrey

"Man it's a great day to be alive"

The next morning while sitting out back eating breakfast I heard a voice say hello. I thought to myself ah oh, I'm in trouble now. It was a pastor of the church; I didn't realize it was Sunday. Sometimes the days seemed like they were all mixed in with one another, just like it was over in Iraq. As we were talking, I asked him was it okay for me to be here, and he said yes that it's no problem. Later on, I found out through our conversation that he was stationed over in Iraq the same year I was there (2004/2005). He was a Native American with an Army hat on and stood about 5 foot 6 inches. He told me that I didn't cover my tracks very well and he said, "After all, I am an Indian from the Zuni tribe. You have to do better than that." He wanted me to meet his family (wife and daughter) in the church. The whole time I talked with them in the church they only had one couple show up for service and they were relatives. They brought some food and I ate a little with them and told them I had to continue on the journey. They seemed very happy and comfortable with each other. It was a nice pretty sunny day to walk. I was headed down Route 191 for St. Johns, Arizona because they had two motels there in town, and my goal was to be in one of them tonight. Back in Vinita, Oklahoma I put on a new pair of Hoka shoes and had not changed them. My dogs (feet) were starting to get very uncomfortable in them now. My feet hurt. I did the mileage from Vinita, to here in St. Johns, Arizona and I got 929 good miles out of this one pair of shoes. Wow, I'm amazed, I wonder if I have walked the furthest in these Hoka shoes before they started breaking down. Meaning would I be the first for the company to do this. The hotel was a good place to rest, get recharged and eat some food at the local diner.

The next morning it was business as usual, walking, and more walking. As I was getting deeper and deeper in Arizona going south to Phoenix, I came upon a sign that said Show Low, Arizona and it had the amount of miles on it to get there. My brain immediately went back to the USDA Forest Service where I worked with a lady by name of Carol Nez that was from Show Low, and she would always talk about living in Show Low with family members. I found this mind blowing how great God is to me that I am able to walk through these places. God is good, all the time.

"It is simply service that measures success." George Washington Carver.

"Man, it's a great day to be alive"

The spirit is allowing me to pull strength from somewhere to do this. I read somewhere the Spirit of God is omnipotent. Meaning having unlimited power; the ability to do anything, which you need no permission to do. And with us being made in the image of God according to the Bible (Genesis 1:27) that same power is within us. That is what blows my mind. I have come to realize I have had this in me my whole life, and so do you. It has taken me 56 years to realize it.

I'm seven months into this walk and it's getting close to Thanksgiving. On this particular day as I was walking, I came upon this housing community that the builders had started and not finished. It had streets and lots. There were no structural houses there and it was totally surrounded by these gray cinderblock walls. There were just empty lots where the houses would go. I could tell that it was going to be a gated community because there was only one way in and one way out. They had the entrance blocked and locked so that no cars or trucks could get in. I was able to maneuver Esmeralda around and under the blockade discreetly as possible. Once in I could move around freely without anyone seeing me. I had a couple of empty lots to choose from. I finally found a good campsite and set up my tent.

It was around November 24th, 2015, close to Thanksgiving. I felt pretty comfortable there because of the walls, but I also felt alone. Just as fast as that thought came to mind a dog appeared and started barking at me from a distance. Wow, count it ALL joy. God listens to your thoughts, and he has a sense of humor (LOL). Now I don't feel so alone. It wasn't a vicious bark, it was more of a curious scared bark. I pulled a part a slice of some turkey lunch meat out of the package. I was sitting there eating my dinner, which consisted of a turkey sandwich with mayo, relish, a little mustard, and powdered milk mixed with some water, Pringle chips, and a squashed Little Debbie Ho Ho cake. I thought I would attempt to maybe hand feed the dog. Negative, my friend, that didn't happen. When I would try to get close to the dog it would keep his distance and continue to bark. I decided to lay the lunch meat on the dirt hill where the dog first appeared and walk back to camp. I watched as the dog came back to that hill and lopped up the meat on the dirt mound, and continued to bark again at me.

"Being confident of this very thing, that He who has begun a good work in you will complete it until the day of Jesus Christ." Philippians 1:6

"Man, it's a great day to be alive"

While leaving Show Low, I pressed on to warmer weather around Phoenix. I walked down this scenic Route 60 into the White Mountain Apache tribe area, which I thought was magnificent. With each curved corner I walked around I had this jaw-dropping experience of the beauty God has made for us. Some of the rocks had such grandeur they were very impressive, mysterious, and overpowering to me. The spirit of peace was in the air, and it felt good.

The day was getting late and I had to find a place to sleep for the night. With all this beauty and ruggedness I knew by looking down onto that forest that it was also very dangerous. When I got past Carrizo, walking up and through the saddles of Bear Mountain which was about 6,424 feet of elevation I found a spot off the side of the road to set up camp. It was a beautiful spot. After I had dinner for the night I sat in my small lightweight chair I got from REI, and watched the sunset. It was something I do every night, that's if it's not raining. While sitting there watching the sunset, I saw these two jets in the distance with the silhouette of the sun beside them flying one behind the other. They had this also beautiful stream of orange jet exhaust that came out the back of them as they were in an upward thrust; man, it was nice looking. It was like a post card.

I finally settled in for the night without a campfire. With the sun completely gone, I zipped up in my tent to get comfortable and relaxed with a movie. Besides, the temperature here was starting to drop. The temperature is supposed to drop down into the high 20s tonight. My tent can be comfortable at times, once inside I can zip up in my sleeping bag. One way I got warm faster in my bag was to just breathe out my mouth a long deep inhale and a long slow exhale. After doing this for a few minutes

I would warm up. My sister gave me this Samsung tablet with six movies and some Gospel music on it. The movies were "Book of Eli" (Denzel Washington), "Good Deeds and I Can do Bad all by Myself" (Tyler Perry), "Joyful Noise" (Queen Latifah), "The Gambler and Contraband" (Mark Wahlberg). The movie I watched the most was the "Tyler Perry" one. On this particular night I had just finished watching "Good Deeds" and as I was turning things off to get ready for bed, I couldn't help but to notice how bright the moonlight radiated outside the tent. So, with me being Curious George, I sat up in my tent and unzipped the entrance flap a quarter of the way down to stick my head out and take a look at the beautiful moonlight. As I did this I must have pulled a little too hard trying to peek outside my tent and one of the poles snapped.

"If you are afraid of failure you don't deserve to be successful!" **Charles Barkley**

"Man, it's a great day to be alive"

I yelled out really loud, "Nooooooooooooooooooooooooo!" It was around 11:30 p.m. Now with half the tent on my head I had a thousand thoughts running through this brain on what to do next. The thought I chose to grab as they flooded through me was Willie T. Clay "The Big Walk" 1960. In his book he talked about walking at night. Now I never spoke out loud about wanting to walk at night, I just entertained the thought by asking myself (just with a thought) *I wonder what it would be like to walk at night.* I thought about the reading from Mr. Clay's book where he walked at night to keep from getting beat up by prejudiced white men. You have to be very, very, very careful of what you think about. Now I knew I would not be able to sleep that night, so I packed up camp under the moonlight/ flashlight. I had made the decision to walk.

It was a little past 12:30 a.m. once getting Esmeralda zipped and snapped down. I knew if I walked from now until around 2 p.m. tomorrow afternoon I would be in town. It would be a 14-hour walk, which I have done twice before, once in Albuquerque (training), and once on this walk back in Ohio to get to a room to watch the NBA playoffs. So, I knew I could do it. As I was walking the winding cliff roads that night I could see in the distance way up high headlights from a truck slowly descending curve after curve. It had to be around four to five miles out there, so the headlights were two little white dots in the distance. I could hear the truck changing gears with each curve it approaches coming down. I kept thinking to myself, "I gotta walk up there." I could not see the road any more than the headlamp would allow me to and I had to turn my head into the direction I wanted to see. There were times as I was walking that night I would look directly down at the road between my forearms as I gripped the handlebar of Esmeralda. With my tunnel vision looking down

270

it looked like a treadmill of asphalt very quickly passing beneath my feet, because that was all I could see with my headlamp. Everything was black dark around me. I would find myself getting this dizzy sick feeling looking down where I had to immediately look up from the road. I think it was from the darkness that surrounded me, and I couldn't see any more than six feet in front of me, I'm not really sure what it was that made me feel that way. I felt like a work horse with blinders on pushing Esmeralda's big heavy girth, at night through these mountain roads here in Arizona. As I continued walking lit up like a Christmas tree with lights flashing on my back side, I would get this eerie feeling that something was watching me. As I walked, I couldn't see anything on either side of me, it was too dark. I had the faith that if I kept the perpetual motion moving forward, I would meet my goals and get through this. I'd been walking now for about three hours and have come to a break in the road where it's about to incline. I stop and take off a layer (cotton hoody) of clothing because I know how much I'm going to sweat pushing Esmeralda up this hill. It is 4 a.m. and my body is tired and starting to really hurt. What hurt the most were my hands and they were burning and stinging from the wetness / coldness of the weather.

"When the goal in front of you becomes more powerful than the obstacles behind you, you will always win." **T.D. Jakes**

"Man, it's a great day to be alive"

My hands were so numb I couldn't even use them to unsnap Esmeralda to get something dry to put on. I was at my lowest point right now wanting to quit. I stopped and tried getting some relief for my hands; they were still wet, cold, stinging/burning, and numb. The negative thought that ran through my mind at that time was, "you have been walking all day, just pull over and rest." It wasn't that easy, my body was wet, cold and tired and my hands would not function. I stood in the middle of the road and cried out, "WHY!" Why am I doing this? Now get this, to put me even further down on that humility pole a person zoomed by angrily blowing their horn at me. I yelled at the driver, "Are you kidding me!" I'm thinking this person has just got out of the bed about an hour ago, had a nice warm shower, has on dry clothes and has the heat on in that car they were driving with their functioning fingers. They're mad at me because they're running late. I've been walking all night. I continued on until morning with the anticipation of warmer weather when the sun comes up. As the skies unzipped the morning light my body started hurting again. This time it was my stomach. It was around 6:30 a.m. and my body is programed to get rid of waste at a certain time each morning. It was that time and I had nowhere to go. Everywhere I looked I would be too conspicuous, and besides my hands were not functioning, they were still burning and numb. I had to painfully keep on walking until some other hurt supersedes this one. The morning was getting brighter and brighter with each step I took, and it was then I could see one of the reasons why I'm doing this. I have a picture of my two granddaughters (Alyiaa and Hazele) taped to the front of Esmeralda looking up at me. They will have a story one day to tell of how their grandfather walked across America, and not one of where he almost walked across America. I think it's all about a good legacy you leave behind. In order to do that, we have to give and help others. This is my way of helping society and I know this helps break the generational curse of leaving behind a bad legacy. I had been walking all night and I had this painful slow lockstep rhythm as I walked, (kinda like the walking dead) I was in a zone. With the morning sun peeking up over the horizon I was feeling not so sleepy. I could see as I looked through my rear-view mirror attached to the left side of Esmeralda a semi-truck approaching me with his four-way flashers on. The truck passed me and pulled over and parked up ahead. The gentleman got out of the truck and met me at the rear of his trailer and said, "Man, it's cold out here." I replied, "You telling me, my hands are cold, wet, and numb." He then asked me what I was doing. I told him that I was walking across America and about my journeys up to this point. He asked me if I needed some help. As I stood there looking at the gentleman the tears in my eyes welled up just before I told him, "yes, I'm hurting, and it's my hands." The gentleman then said, "I saw you around 2 a.m. this morning as I was making a milk delivery run." He went on to say that his son is in the Army and has left for Kuwait yesterday. "I see you are a veteran and I'm going to help you."

There is no exercise better for the heart than reaching down and lifting people up." **John Holmes**

"Man, it's a great day to be alive"

We loaded up Big Esmeralda into the semi-trailer with his hydraulic lift and tied her down, which he had to do for me. My hands were still sore. I got in the cab of the truck with the gentleman and we had a great life conversation, talking about almost everything. He had some warm cocoa to drink and heat coming out of the vents. This felt so, so good. He stopped at the first place that served food and picked something up for us. We finally arrived at a hotel and this gentleman insisted on paying for my room for two nights and I ended up staying three nights instead. This man was Godsend to me. The down time allowed my body to heal and I ordered a tent. While communicating with my cousin Shelia Morton from Indiana (the one that said stop and smell the flowers) she told me her nephew lives near the area I was in. I had never met this cousin, but I knew his father who passed away back in 1980. He was the same age as me and we visited one another a lot as kids. There's that word again: serendipitous. It makes me think back to one of the ladies I met in Pennsylvania at a book luncheon. She said that I would experience the natural gift for discovery the whole entire journey, so get ready and hang on. I met my cousin (Kenyon) and his wife and child when they came by the hotel to give me a ride to pick up a new tent. Man, I thank God for this blessing. The next day I continued on towards Surprise, Arizona to visit a retired Postal friend Jake and Maureen (Mo) Blalock. They put me up for a few days and it was really good seeing them. They were very kind to me, and they helped and it was much appreciated. It was good reminiscing about the years past working at the Post Office and now I'm headed to Buckeye. As Esmeralda and I put on the miles heading southwest we walked alongside this cotton field and to my ignorance I somehow never thought cotton would be this far west of the Mississippi River. This is a thought that I'd had all my life up until today. Sure enough, it's cotton. I saw cotton bales as tall, wide and long as annex containers on the side of the road awaiting pick-up. My parents and other elders have told many of stories about making weight with cotton bags and just picking it. I can remember a time when my dad would explain the difference from picking and chopping cotton. I had to stop Esmeralda, pull over and pick one of the cotton's seed pods. Esmeralda was as excited as I was to actually see something that I had read about all my life. The sharp, flat, hard pointy leaf that cradles the cotton ball like a catcher's baseball mitt sticks and it hurts when your fingertips jam down onto them. Man, this is mind blowing to know that my forefathers and mothers had to do this all day long without pay and were punished and made an example of if the cotton bag at the end of the day did not meet weight. I thank God for those days, and I thank God for these days because they have made me who I am today. The lineage of my ancestors makes me very strong and enduring. I am ever so grateful to be from the line of the descent that make up my family. As I continued my westward way down this Route 85 toward Gila Bend, Arizona, I found a place in Gila Bend to sleep and to think about how I was going to continue my journeys across these United States.

"In life, winning and losing will both happen. What is never acceptable is quitting." **Magic Johnson**

<u>What Arizona means to me</u>
Arizona, Arizona with its hot desert climate
Brings snowbirds and visitors
That are not on assignments
The Grand Canyon state is beautiful indeed
With desert sand dunes
That will bring you to your knees
Rugged, hard, hot weather and cold
I must keep pushing Esmeralda
To hit my goal

Chapter 13

California

"Man, it's a great day to be alive"

My Global Positioning System (GPS) on my phone wants me to take a journey across the border to Sonoyta, Mexico. I am not walking into Mexico. I will have to walk on Interstate 8 southwest to Chula Vista, California. While walking down I-8 west I knew I would encounter a state trooper and I did. We met and he introduced himself and I did likewise. The officer was very professional, kind, polite, and kosher. He asked for my driver's license and I handed it to him. Then he told me that I can't walk on the Interstate, and he said in most cases I would give you a ride, but since you're pushing Esmeralda he advised me to be vigilant and stay focused on my way to Chula Vista. As I kept on pushing on, I walked through the Winterhaven, California area on I-8 southwest and I heard this dark four-door truck blow at me like they knew me and yelled out the passenger side window, "Hey, TONY!" I said to myself who is this person, a Facebook follower wanting to talk and take a picture, like it happened earlier in the walk? No, it was Reanetta Siquieros a former USDA co-worker sister Janelle and her husband Manny with their children Isabelle, Angelina, and Ava going to Disneyland in Anaheim, for family vacation. Wow, mind-blowing, what are the chances, there's that word again, serendipitous, occurring by chance in a happy and beneficial way. I would also like to acknowledge God for creating the whole situation that's happening. Mr. Manny and his family gave me a ride around 18 miles down the road to Gordon's Well RV Park off of I-8sw. It was really good seeing them; it brought back memories of me celebrating New Year's Eve (2009) with them down in Tucson, Arizona. They are really great people.

"Happiness cannot be traveled to, owned, earned, worn or consumed. Happiness is the spiritual experience living every minute with Love, Grace, and Gratitude." Denis Waitley

"Man, it's a great day to be alive"

I made it to Calexico, California and started to get a little tired of walking every day for 20 miles or so. I was walking on this road under construction which had no shoulders. I had to walk in the road for a little under a mile with traffic behind me. I had traffic backed up and there was a big semi dump truck behind me that couldn't go around me. I could tell that he was getting a little aggravated with me walking and at the speed I was walking. Each time he would pull down on the horn and it would give out a quick short loud burp (telling me to move over) I would throw up my arms as I'm walking with my back to him to say, "Where am I going, the shoulders are cut off and it's a small dropout." I'm not going to risk injuring Esmeralda or myself, but this guy in the truck behind me was aggravating me now. Finally, there was a break and the traffic was able to go around me and the truck driver pulled down on his horn one last time in passing Esmeralda and I.

I was able to actually walk a Border Patrol checkpoint which made for interesting conversation once it was my turn to go through the checkpoint. I had to stand there in line in back of cars and trucks in front of me so everybody around me were looking and wondering what I was doing. This was the same question the Border Patrol officer asked me (what are you doing). The closer I got to complete this westward journey, the sadder I got. I kept thinking what next, or would I continue this high with this accomplishment. The other thought that ran through my mind was that of I have to get back into the mainstream of doing things like paying bills and just talking to people. This route near Jacumba, California takes me really close to the US/Mexican border wall. I can see the wall as I walk along the road. Today during my lunch break I sat behind an old shed on someone's property thinking about my next move and how much further would I walk before finding a place to camp for the night. Then out of nowhere a Border Patrol helicopter appeared and hovered overhead looking down at me. I could see an officer sitting in the open side door with his feet hanging trying to see whether or not I was a person crossing over from Mexico. I stood up and started waving up to the chopper and the crew. They eventually left. Another thing that I was really concerned about was meeting up with someone who was crossing over into the United States. I wondered if they would be friendly or would I have to fight someone. I made it to Barrett Junction and today it started to rain. On top of that I came upon this house with three big, brown, vicious healthy bloodhounds with no fence and no one came outside. I pulled out my police baton and whacked it on the ground a couple of times letting them know I was not afraid of them. I just kept walking with confidence and walked right out of their so-called guarded territory. I'm so close I can smell the ocean water and can see the light at the end of the tunnel. Chula Vista Imperial Beach here I come. I had made a hotel reservation the night before and I told the guy that I was walking and would be there today.

"To love someone is nothing, to be loved by someone is something, to love someone who loves you is everything." **Bill Russell**

"Man, it's a great day to be alive"

He said okay and that he would have a room for me. I got there and he had no rooms available. He told me that he was sorry, and he wanted to give me ten dollars for my cause. I told him to keep the money, I don't want it. I called Legacy Church in Albuquerque and they helped me get a better hotel right on the beach for two nights. God is good All the time. I had to wait for my Uncle Joe, my dad's childhood friend, a retired CIA employee who lives in Southern California, and a film crew (Cody and Britta) from Legacy Church. They wanted to film me walking onto the beach and crossing the finish line. The president of the San Diego Make-A-Wish foundation (Chris Sichel) showed up alone with Phil Harris, Charlie and Elaine Lane, Rebecca Martinez, and Joe Tucker Sr. to hold the finish line ribbon. It was a bittersweet feeling knowing I had to stop because my body was tired and I had no more roads to walk. Man, 244 days ago I was putting my feet into the Atlantic Ocean and today I'm putting the same two feet into the Pacific Ocean. I did it one step at a time. I met some people on the journey who would always tell me how to walk across America. Someone told me one time that to see the real beauty of America you can't experience what's truly out there if you are in a hotel at night. Well, I'm here to tell you they are wrong. Sometimes I needed the hot showers, solitude of four walls, the cleanliness of some rooms, and the ability to just walk around nude. For me it also gave me down time and to let the physical body catch up with the mind. By far the most memorable experience would be going; *"Out for a walk"*.

<u>What California means to me</u>
California, California
My journey is over, My walk is done,
Now it's time to give thanks to the Great One,
God took me through peace, happiness, sorrow, and pain,
With this combination, the world don't look the same,
The Great I AM is for me and you,
We just have to open our eyes to see Him true.
Gratitude, empathy, and Love,
Goes together like a hand in a glove.
It's something we're born with, and not something we buy,
We just have you keep our hands and heads to the sky.
Giving thanks and given thanks

THE END

REFERENCE

Read more at: https://www.brainyquote.com/topics/good_day

Read more at: https://www.brainyquote.com/topics/courageous

Read more at: https://www.brainyquote.com/quotes/topics/topic_thankful.html

Read more at: https://www.brainyquote.com/quotes/quotes/c/condoleezz453866.html?src=t_great_things

Read more at: https://www.brainyquote.com/quotes/quotes/j/jankaron489877.html?src=t_good_people

Read more at: https://www.brainyquote.com/topics/good_person

Printed in the United States
By Bookmasters